W9-CME-419

Mindfulness for Children

150+ Mindfulness Activities for Happier, Healthier, Stress-Free Kids

TRACY L. DANIEL, PHD

Adams Media
New York London Toronto Sydney New Delhi

Adams Media
An Imprint of Simon & Schuster, Inc.
57 Littlefield Street
Avon, Massachusetts 02322

Copyright © 2018 by Simon & Schuster, Inc.

All rights reserved, including the right to reproduce this book or portions thereof in any form whatsoever. For information address Adams Media Subsidiary Rights Department, 1230 Avenue of the Americas, New York, NY 10020.

First Adams Media trade paperback edition September 2018

ADAMS MEDIA and colophon are trademarks of Simon & Schuster.

For information about special discounts for bulk purchases, please contact Simon & Schuster Special Sales at 1-866-506-1949 or business@simonandschuster.com.

The Simon & Schuster Speakers Bureau can bring authors to your live event. For more information or to book an event contact the Simon & Schuster Speakers Bureau at 1-866-248-3049 or visit our website at www.simonspeakers.com.

Interior design by Michelle Kelly
Interior illustration by Nicola Dos Santos

Manufactured in the United States of America

10 9 8 7 6 5 4 3 2 1

Library of Congress Cataloging-in-Publication Data
Daniel, Tracy L., author.
Mindfulness for children / Tracy L. Daniel, PhD.
Avon, Massachusetts: Adams Media, 2018.
Includes bibliographical references and index.
LCCN 2018017351 (print) | LCCN 2018021819 (ebook) | ISBN 9781507208137 (pb) | ISBN 9781507208144 (ebook)
Subjects: LCSH: Cognitive therapy for children. | Meditation--Therapeutic use. | Child psychotherapy. | BISAC: FAMILY & RELATIONSHIPS / Parenting / General. | BODY, MIND & SPIRIT / Meditation. | BODY, MIND & SPIRIT / Reference.
Classification: LCC RJ505.C63 (ebook) | LCC RJ505.C63 D36 2018 (print) | DDC 618.92/891425--dc23
LC record available at https://lccn.loc.gov/2018017351

ISBN 978-1-5072-0813-7
ISBN 978-1-5072-0814-4 (ebook)

This book is intended as general information only and should not be used to diagnose or treat any health condition. In light of the complex, individual, and specific nature of health problems, this book is not intended to replace professional medical advice. The ideas, procedures, and suggestions in this book are intended to supplement, not replace, the advice of a trained medical professional. Consult your physician before adopting any of the suggestions in this book, as well as about any condition that may require diagnosis or medical attention. The author and publisher disclaim any liability arising directly or indirectly from the use of this book.

Many of the designations used by manufacturers and sellers to distinguish their products are claimed as trademarks. Where those designations appear in this book and Simon & Schuster, Inc., was aware of a trademark claim, the designations have been printed with initial capital letters.

This publication is designed to provide accurate and authoritative information with regard to the subject matter covered. It is sold with the understanding that the publisher is not engaged in rendering legal, accounting, or other professional advice. If legal advice or other expert assistance is required, the services of a competent professional person should be sought.
—From a *Declaration of Principles* jointly adopted by a Committee of the American Bar Association and a Committee of Publishers and Associations

The information in this book should not be used for diagnosing or treating any health problem. Not all diet and exercise plans suit everyone. You should always consult a trained medical professional before starting a diet, taking any form of medication, or embarking on any fitness or weight-training program. The author and publisher disclaim any liability arising directly or indirectly from the use of this book.

Contents

Foreword

Children play. It is their nature to play. When mindfulness for children engages them in a fun, playful way, they will be drawn into their own natural focus and calm. Mindfulness will always be relevant for their lives because they can use its tools—awareness of breath, movement, and stillness—anywhere along their life path.

Dr. Tracy Daniel knows this. She has dedicated her career to creatively adapting meditative experiences into fun activities for children. Among her many stellar qualifications is one with which I am particularly familiar, and that I find sprinkled throughout this wonderful book: her work as a certified teacher of Radiant Child Yoga.

When I began teaching children yoga and mindfulness several decades ago, I noticed something remarkable: children had a much easier time than adults in learning to be present...being mindful in the moment. I found that I became more present to the "here and now" when I was with children. I know that Tracy has experienced this, too. It is one of the reasons she has devoted her life to children. She wants to help them stay connected, present, and mindful of themselves. And just like me, she has noticed that purposeful play is the key method. Within these pages you will find one creative activity after another that will allow you and your children to enjoy purposeful play together.

Prepare to discover a multitude of mindful activities in these pages: meditations, yoga movements, games, art projects, guided relaxations, and much more. Tracy's clear and practical style makes it easy to jump right in with your children in tow, with all of you becoming more mindful, joyful, calm, and connected to yourselves and each other. I'm so happy to see a Radiant Child Yoga trainer like Tracy bringing these gifts to families, teachers, and, most of all, to the beautiful souls we call children!

Shakta Khalsa
Founder of Radiant Child Yoga
ERYT-500, Author, Montessori Educator
ChildrensYoga.com

Acknowledgments

I am so very grateful to the many individuals who have indirectly and directly contributed to this book. I want to express my sincerest gratitude to my yoga and mindfulness mentors, for without their knowledge and expertise this mindfulness journey would not have been possible. I'd first like to thank Angie Eckenroth, who introduced this marathon runner to the amazing benefits of yoga. Angie has been a phenomenal yoga resource, mentor, and friend throughout the years. Shakta Khalsa, for showing me how to teach yoga and meditation to children. Shakta is one of the most inspirational individuals I have ever met. Lindsey Thomas Lieneck, for sharing her occupational therapy, mindfulness, and aerial yoga knowledge. Lindsey has been an invaluable resource for my aerial yoga business. These women have shaped my personal mindfulness practice, my work with children, and my business practices. I am forever grateful for the knowledge, wisdom, and philosophy they have shared with me.

To my occupational therapy friends who have taught me so much over the years regarding sensory processing, movement, and motor planning. In my early years when I was a psychologist, Traci Ridder, an occupational therapist, taught me a great deal about how sensory processing relates to behavior. This shaped my psychological practice and taught me to engage a wider perspective on well-being than I had learned in graduate school. Thank you, Traci.

I also owe a great deal of gratitude to my good friend, Deana Lesher, who has not only taught me the importance of primitive reflexes, but took the time to review and edit the Mindfulness and the Senses chapter to make sure it was complementary with an occupational therapy approach. Thank you so much!

Thank you to my amazing team at Mindful Child Aerial Yoga. I have a fabulous team of professionals working for me, including my daughter, Kennedy Myers. This project wouldn't have been possible without their enduring commitment to children. I am truly blessed to have such a great team.

To my partner and best friend, Travis Heimer, for being so understanding while I wrote this book. I am so grateful for your continued support, suggestions, and positive encouragement. You helped me to persevere with running my business while writing this book. Thank you!

My deepest thanks to my sisters, Tami Daniel, Mallory Daniel, and Kristen Galle. To my brother, Zachary Daniel; my uncles, Terry Jett and Dave Walters; and my parents, Scott and Diane Daniel, thank you so much for your positive encouragement, understanding, and help throughout my life and the writing process.

I appreciate the support and assistance of the Simon & Schuster editors and staff, who made this project possible. Thank you, Julia Jacques and Laura Daly, for your patience and guidance in helping me figure out how to write a book.

Introduction

We all want our children to be able to focus when necessary, calm themselves down if they're upset, and bounce back from disappointments. But how exactly do you teach kids these skills? The answer is *mindfulness*, the practice of quieting your mind and focusing on the present moment. The same practice that is being taught in the adult world is also useful for children.

Just as adults deal with worries, stress, and challenges, so do children. Teaching them mindfulness will enable them to deal with these emotions in a balanced, healthy way. Science has shown time and again the myriad benefits of methods such as mindfulness and yoga for physical and mental health. Providing mindfulness strategies and ways to cope with stress early in life gives children a chance to build resilience so they can meet life's daily challenges. What's even more amazing is that it is simple, doesn't take long, and is relatively inexpensive. Implementing a few minutes of paying attention in the moment and breathing can really make a difference in your child's life! This age-old practice for connecting the brain, body, and mind can have a tremendous impact on children's health and well-being.

From my perspective as a mental health professional, yoga instructor, and parent, I have seen the effects mindful awareness can have on strengthening kids' minds. This book will show you some of the mindfulness practices that I use in my classes with children. The activities are backed by scientific research, and I can personally attest to their effectiveness and, most important, the fun and delight they bring to children. In fact, kids love these exercises so much, I can't get them to leave after our classes end! This guide provides you with these techniques so you can instill in your children the same happiness, resilience, and pure joy that I see in children daily.

PART ONE

Mindfulness Basics

Welcome to the beginning of your child's mindfulness journey! You'll learn the definition of *mindfulness* and what a practice of mindfulness for children entails. Are you wondering exactly how mindfulness can change your child's health and well-being? You'll learn how in this part. Finally, we'll discuss proper breathing techniques and how to teach mindfulness to children, which is very different from teaching adults. Get ready to witness the powerful ways that mindfulness provides children with a sense of calm, a focused mind, and a happier outlook on life.

CHAPTER 1

An Introduction to Mindfulness

This chapter introduces the history of mindfulness and what modern science tells us are the benefits of a mindfulness practice. Cutting-edge research in the areas of neuroscience, psychology, and mindfulness shows us how a mindfulness practice of just ten minutes a day can change how your child feels!

What Is Mindfulness?

Mindfulness is an English word that means "focused, sustained attention, in a nonjudgmental manner, to the here and now." It is the process of using your senses to pay attention to your internal and external experiences in the present moment. Mindfulness can take many forms. It can be a yoga practice, breath work, walking, coloring, or even martial arts. All mindfulness practices share a focus on sharpening attention and building self-regulation skills to handle challenging situations. Some practices, like the ones offered in this book, emphasize empathy, kindness, gratitude, and compassion. Mindfulness principles can also be applied to everyday life and incorporated into daily activities, such as eating, brushing your teeth, and simply breathing.

A Brief History of Mindfulness

Mindfulness has been practiced for thousands of years and different practitioners have referred to it by different names. Mindfulness is closely related to yoga and meditation.

Its recent rise in popularity in the United States is the result of an intersection of science and anectodal evidence. As yoga, meditation, and mindfulness gained attention in our society, psychologists, physicians, and other professionals began practicing. Many immediately recognized the benefits of stress reduction and health promotion. They began collecting data on their experiences, which provided evidence of the positive effects of mindfulness.

Jon Kabat-Zinn, professor of medicine emeritus at the University of Massachusetts Medical School, is widely credited as being a pioneer in making mindfulness accessible to a wide audience. Kabat-Zinn studied meditation under influential Buddhist teachers. He combined what he learned from Buddhism with Western science to develop his Mindfulness-Based Stress Reduction (MBSR) program (which is secular, meaning free from religious ties). This and other integrations of meditation methods with science helped to bring mindfulness to the attention of professionals who are familiar with science-based interventions. Thus Western science confirmed what the practitioners in the East had known for years—mindfulness can make people feel calmer and happier.

Why Mindfulness for Kids?

For children, mindfulness is defined as the practice of paying attention, with your senses, in a kind way, so you can choose your behavior. Childhood is full of fun and play, sure—but kids everywhere also experience stress, anxiety, challenging situations, and overstimulation from time to time. Yet knowing how to deal with these obstacles is *not* an innate skill that most kids have.

Teaching your children mindfulness can help promote emotional balance and protect them from the harmful effects of chronic stress. Mindfulness teaches children about their inner and outer worlds, which makes them aware of their emotions. Mindfulness shows children how to overcome challenges through guided instruction in fun, sensory-based activities. Children learn to identify thoughts and emotions and relate them to experiences through games, movement, breathing, and art activities. Simple mindfulness practices like the ones in this book keep children engaged and help them to reduce stress, improve concentration, and handle difficult emotions.

Mindfulness is also appealing for children because it provides a holistic approach to living that addresses the entire child:

- Mindfulness **nurtures children's health** by building habits of mind and behavior that create resilience for today's fast-paced world.
- Mindfulness **teaches children to be flexible**, manage their feelings, navigate difficult situations without becoming overwhelmed, and much more.

- Mindfulness **fosters the ability to become more connected to the body, emotions, and mind**. When children are more connected to their emotions, they can make better choices about how they respond to the world around them.

As a parent or caregiver, it is difficult to know how to help children learn the social and emotional skills they need to be successful in school and life. Mindfulness is a great place to start—it's a tool that children can use throughout life to navigate daily demands with reflection instead of reactivity.

The Science of Mindfulness

How does mindfulness work, in scientific terms? Can it actually change the brain and the way you react to situations? The answer is yes. In recent years, there has been an explosion of research showing that mindfulness practice can change the function and the structure of the brain. Science even demonstrates which parts of the brain are affected by mindfulness practice and how these amazing changes can benefit our minds and bodies. Here are some ways that mindfulness impacts your brain, and subsequently your well-being:

- **Mindfulness can change the brain for the better.** Recent studies using brain-imaging techniques have shown positive changes in brain structure and activity after participation in mindfulness practices. The images indicated greater blood flow and a thickening of the cerebral cortex in areas linked with attention and emotions. The research has also shown that the changes in participants' brains corresponded to the number of hours they spent practicing mindfulness. The more they practiced, the more the brain changed. The brain's ability to adapt is called *neuroplasticity*, meaning the brain has pliability and can change with experience. A consistent practice of mindfulness can create new pathways in the brain, resulting in improved mental health, physical health, and well-being.
- **Mindfulness keeps our brains young.** Sara Lazar, a neuroscientist at Harvard Medical School, found that mindfulness can keep your brain from shrinking as you age. Research demonstrates that the cortex shrinks as you age, but the prefrontal cortex of fifty-year-old mindfulness practitioners had the same amount of gray matter as those who were twenty-five years old. Furthermore,

this was true for individuals who had been practicing mindfulness for only eight weeks. Just imagine the benefits that children's brains are receiving by learning a mindfulness practice early in life!

- **Mindfulness increases resiliency.** Electrical changes have been noted in the left frontal portion of the brain following mindfulness training, which scientists believe is linked to enhanced resilience. Resilience is the ability to cope in challenging situations and bounce back from adversity. Mindful children can deal with difficult emotions without shutting down and are able to bounce back quicker from disappointment.
- **Mindfulness can be a valuable addition to many traditional treatment plans.** Mindfulness has been shown to grow gray matter in regions of the brain that are responsible for higher-level cognitive skills, also known as executive functioning. A study at the UCLA Mindful Awareness Research Center (MARC) found that adolescents with attentional problems demonstrated improved executive function after participation in mindfulness classes.
- **Mindfulness keeps us healthy.** Another benefit of regular mindfulness practice is that it enhances the body's ability to fight off infection. How does mindfulness improve the immune system? Mindfulness reduces stress and encourages relaxation—this, in turn, reduces harmful stress hormones, which produce inflammation in the body. Chronic stress and inflammation lead to illness and can have serious detrimental effects on overall health.
- **Mindfulness strengthens sensory regions of the brain.** Lazar also found increased gray matter in sensory and auditory regions of the brain, and decreases in the amygdala. The amygdala is a lower brain center responsible for "fight, flight, or freeze" responses to stress. When you practice mindfulness, you are paying attention to your senses, listening to sounds, and focusing on breathing. When you are in the present moment, you grow gray matter in sensory regions and rely on calm decision-making processes instead of knee-jerk reactions.

What Are the Benefits of Mindfulness for Children?

There are myriad ways that mindfulness can improve anyone's overall well-being. But what are some benefits specific to children's daily lives? First, mindfulness activities are great for kids because they:

- Are easy to introduce.
- Take little time to implement.
- Are inexpensive.
- Can be done anytime and anywhere. (The mindfulness strategies in this book are perfect for home, school, and public places.)
- Are fun! Incorporating fun enhances the learning process and helps kids learn the skill faster.

Beyond these logistics, mindfulness offers countless benefits for kids' bodies and minds. Let's look more in depth at some of the physical and mental benefits of mindfulness in children.

Executive Functioning

Executive function is a term that encompasses a range of skills—working memory, perspective-taking, decision-making, emotional regulation, problem-solving, planning, and impulse control. It provides the foundation for all educational and social activities. When children are under stress, it is harder for them to access executive functioning skills to make wise decisions. If the stress they experience is chronic, executive function can be more seriously impaired, leading to problems with learning, memory impairment, and behavior issues.

Science has proved that mindfulness practice can strenghten executive functioning. That's because repeated mindfulness practice actually builds neural pathways in the brain, and these create habits and automatic responses. A consistent mindfulness practice changes neural pathways to neural superhighways, making executive functioning more accessible to children in times of stress. For example, say that a classmate takes a toy from your child. Instead of yelling and grabbing it back (which might be prompted by an old neural pathway), your child may instead automatically refer to a mindfulness practice and take deep breaths before asking if they can have back the toy that they were using.

Here are some of the recognized benefits that mindfulness can provide for your child's executive functioning:

- Improves working memory (temporary storage and managing of information to carry out cognitive tasks)
- Reduces impulsivity

- Promotes planning and organization skills
- Develops ability to initiate and monitor one's own actions
- Encourages cognitive flexibility (considering other points of view)
- Builds emotional intelligence (the ability to notice and manage one's own emotions)
- Enhances skills that lead to thoughtful decision-making

Mental Health

Simple mindfulness strategies like the ones in this book can provide children with tools to assist them in counteracting any stress, distractions, and anxiety they encounter in their daily lives. Numerous studies have even demonstrated that children with a variety of conditions—such as depression, anxiety, attention-deficit hyperactivity disorder, and eating disorders—benefit from practicing mindfulness. Science has shown that well-conducted mindfulness practices can reduce the symptoms of these conditions and help children be calm, resilient, and happy.

Here are some of the recognized benefits that mindfulness can provide for your child's mental health:

- Reduces anxiety and stress
- Improves attention and focus
- Decreases negative self-belief
- Enhances happiness
- Eases symptoms of depression
- Helps overcome somatic symptoms (physical symptoms caused by psychological problems)
- Stimulates mindful self-awareness
- Improves social and emotional skills
- Develops the ability to manage difficult emotions
- Decreases hyperactivity and aggression
- Improves behavior regulation
- Reduces reactivity and encourages reflection
- Improves relaxation and calmness
- Relieves fears and feelings of helplessness
- Balances high and low energy levels

Always talk to your child's healthcare providers about the most effective way to manage his or her specific conditions.

Well-Being

Mindfulness also has beneficial effects on overall well-being in children. Science has shown that just ten minutes a day of mindfulness practice can produce an impact on children's well-being fairly quickly. Every child is different—kids will pick up new skills with each activity, and within a few months they'll have a complete toolbox that they can access in difficult times.

Here are some of the recognized benefits that mindfulness can provide for your child's well-being:

- Improves self-esteem
- Supports attainment of personal goals
- Enhances empathy, optimism, persistence, and resiliency
- Promotes development of social relationships
- Creates self-connection and self-awareness
- Expands connection with nature

A consistent practice with your child will cultivate positive life skills, such as adaptability, kindness, and gratitude.

Learning

Mindfulness can even play a role in the development of cognitive and academic skills. The improvements in academic ability and cognitive thinking are linked to the enrichment of executive functioning skills. Mindfulness helps children focus on the skills needed to initiate an assignment, organize their work, remember the steps required to finish their tasks, and complete their project. When children are mindful they are able to prioritize, stick with difficult problems, avoid distractions, and not become frustrated.

Here's how mindfulness can benefit your child's learning. Mindfulness:

- Expands metacognition (essentially, thinking about thinking).
- Improves academic performance.
- Eases test anxiety.
- Enhances creativity.
- Leads to a more effective utilization of knowledge.
- Enriches reasoning skills and clarity.

- Improves posture, which assists with fine motor tasks, such as writing.
- Promotes better work habits and cooperation.
- Increases school attendance rate.

A lot of factors impact academic achievement, but mindfulness practice is likely to offer children some go-to techniques that can apply to the way they approach work throughout their lives.

Physical Health

Research has shown that mindfulness can help children stay healthy and make better health-related decisions. Mindfulness around eating and nutritional choices can especially impact a child's physical health, now and later as an adult.

When it comes to your child's health, studies show that mindfulness:

- Lowers blood pressure
- Improves digestion and elimination
- Strengthens the immune system
- Promotes better sleep
- Helps chronic illness
- Increases body awareness and motor planning
- Enhances sensory integration
- Reduces stress hormones, such as cortisol

You'll find an entire chapter of mindfulness exercises in this book devoted to mindful eating.

Mindful Breathing

Before we delve into specific activities, it's important to learn the basics of mindful breathing. No matter what activity you and your children choose, it helps to remember to use mindful breathing while you do it.

Did you know that breathing has positive effects on multiple systems in the body? For example, fast breathing styles tend to excite our nervous system while slow breathing calms it. Contrary to popular belief, the pace of your breathing has nothing to do with getting more oxygen into the body. The key aspect to think about is actually carbon dioxide. Scientists have demonstrated that slow, deep breathing results in higher levels of carbon dioxide in the blood. These higher levels of carbon dioxide increase the blood flow to the brain, which means the brain gets more oxygen. This build-up of carbon dioxide (to a safe level, of course) also slows metabolism, resulting in a pleasant, calm feeling. In addition:

- Researchers have also found that mindful breathing calms the body by reducing blood pressure, improving concentration, and slowing the heart rate.
- Focusing on breathing is associated with enhanced functioning in the higher brain regions. Mindful breathing reduces anxiety by short-circuiting the "fight, flight, or freeze" response that occurs in the lower brain centers. Controlled breathing allows children to think before they react, which results in behavior that is reflective.
- Mindful breathing teaches children that they have control over how they feel, which is something most children do not realize. Mindful breathing allows children to have power over their physical and mental energy, which, in turn, teaches them to self-regulate and engage in mindful behavior.

Tips for Mindful Breathing

You might think that breathing is automatic—and to a great extent, it is. But you can teach your children (and yourself) to breathe mindfully using these strategies:

- **Sit or stand up tall.** Mindful breathing can be practiced sitting, standing, or lying down. The key is for children to be relaxed in whatever posture they choose. If sitting or standing, roll the shoulders up by the ears and let them drop down the back, open the chest through the heart, and push the shoulders back and down. Creating a good posture maximizes the effects of mindful breathing.
- **Breathe slowly.** Slowing the breath initiates the relaxation response. When you teach children to breathe slowly and extend the exhale, they begin to become aware that it changes how they feel. Slow, relaxed breathing has a positive effect on multiple systems in the body that control how we feel. Breathing slowly from the diaphragm affects sleep, memory, energy level, and focus.
- **Breathe through the nose.** In mindful breathing, children should breathe through the nose unless otherwise instructed (this will be discussed in a later breathing exercise). When we breathe in through the nose, it plays an important role as

it warms, moisturizes, and prepares the air for the lungs. The membranes in the nose also clean the air to ward off viruses. The nasal passage slows the breathing rate, prolongs the exhalation, and is more efficient for the lungs and heart. Breathing through the nose also requires greater focus, which helps children stay connected to their body when breath is linked to movement.

- **Breathe from the belly, not the chest.** Babies fill their bellies with air completely every time they inhale and exhale, but somewhere along the way this calm, healing style is lost and shallow breathing is substituted. Shallow, partial breathing can result in decreased focus, low energy, and heightened anxiety.
- **Pause.** Healthy, relaxed breathing has pauses at the end of the exhale and inhale. When children are under stress, they tend to lose the pauses. Children should first be taught to breathe without pausing or holding their breath. Children may at first not understand the difference between pausing and retaining or holding their breath. This may result in added stress or strain if they try to hold their breath. The pause should happen as a natural result of the relaxation response, not an intentional holding of the breath.
- **Know which exercises to use.** Some breathing exercises can be energizing and others are calming. Depending on your child and your intention, it is important to be familiar with the effects of the breathing exercises in order to make the best choice, depending on the situation. For example, avoid or minimize the energizing breathing exercises when children are already overactive.
- **Designate a place.** Mindfulness and mindful breathing can be practiced anywhere, but it may be helpful for children to designate a place where they can "chillax" or take a "brain break." This space needs to be dimly lit and comfortable. It doesn't need to be large—just offer enough room for children to be able to lie down or sit. Aerial yoga hammocks are especially calming to children due to the sensory input they provide via evenly distributed deep pressure on the skin. Mindful breathing can be enhanced in an aerial hammock as it provides a quiet, distraction-free experience for children.
- **Practice.** Mindful breathing is like any skill—it takes practice. Incorporating even a short daily practice can change your child's brain. As children practice breathing mindfully, their brains create new connections or neural pathways. With repeated practice and experience, the brain makes a pathway that is frequently used, which reinforces the habit of responding to stress with mindful breathing.

Mindful breathing will no doubt help your child with the exercises in this book and throughout his or her entire life!

How Do You Teach Mindfulness to Children?

Any parent or caregiver knows that it is difficult for children to be still for any length of time and some find it hard to calm down—so simply telling kids to sit still and be calm isn't going to work. The best elementary school teachers know how to present information to children in a manner that is infused with movement, fun, and play, so children are more likely to retain it. The same methods can be used for teaching mindfulness to children.

Children learn through their senses. Activities that are multisensory and include movement are the most engaging and are the easiest way to teach mindfulness. Attention to your senses gives you an immediate experience of the present moment. Your brain focuses on the mindfulness activity instead of worrying about the future or ruminating about the past.

Finally, use fun activities, like the ones in this book! Adele Diamond, a professor of developmental cognitive neuroscience at the University of British Columbia, found that when we engage in activities we find enjoyable, our brain produces dopamine, a neurotransmitter that gets our brain primed for peak performance. This means mindfulness activities should be fun, full of movement, multisensory, and play-based!

How to Use This Book

This book is a tool you and your child can use together to develop a mindfulness practice.

Be a Positive Role Model!

While there is no right or wrong way to use this book, it is important that *you* first understand what mindfulness is, and start to cultivate a practice of your own before trying to teach it to your child. The best way to understand mindfulness is by doing it. Practice is necessary to become familiar with mindfulness activities. Experience the techniques yourself, especially in the next two chapters, before teaching them to your child. Your personal experience with mindfulness is the key to being ready to teach others these activities.

There are a couple of reasons for practicing and becoming familiar with the techniques before implementing them with your child:

1. It will ensure that you are able to teach them anytime you need to, without having to grab the book and read through the instructions. If you are a visual learner and want to see a picture of some of the poses, mudras, or activities in this book, visit the Mindful Child Aerial Yoga website at www.mindfulchildaerialyoga.com and click on the "Blog" tab.

2. *Mindfulness* is more than a buzzword; it is a way of life that teaches children to quiet and focus their minds, to be healthy, and to be kind to themselves and others. Noticing when you are acting in a mindless manner, slowing down, and developing mindfulness in your life takes practice. Even those of us who have been practicing it for years still find that our busy lives get the best of us; we do tasks while lost in a fog, and sometimes are not sure how we completed them. Set aside a few minutes each day to practice being mindful so that it can become your lifestyle. You are doing the dishes, brushing your teeth, and walking the dog anyway, so why not do it mindfully?

Understanding How the Activities Are Set Up

Once you have a good handle on practicing mindfulness yourself, you can begin using these activities with your child. The activities in Chapter 2 are focused on mindful movement. It is an important chapter as the movements and poses are utilized throughout the rest of the book. Chapter 3 introduces breathing exercises that are calming and energizing, along with games and breathing props. Read Chapters 2 and 3 first. They are the foundation upon which all the other chapters are built. After you have read these two chapters, you will know enough about poses, movement, and breath work to decide which other chapters will be most helpful for your child.

Chapters 4 through 9 teach techniques for mindfulness that have different focuses and specific effects:

- **The seven senses:** This section includes lessons for sensory integration, which are energizing and calming.
- **Eating mindfully:** This chapter explains fun ways to incorporate healthy, mindful eating habits into your child's life.
- **Focus, concentration, and attention:** These activities will help your child improve focus without realizing he or she is doing it.

- **Mudras, mind-sets, and positive affirmations:** A mudra (pronounced "moo-drah") is a symbol your child makes with his or her hands and fingers that can help with focus, relaxation, or energy. Mind-sets teach children that with effort and persistence they can grow their cognitive ability. Positive affirmations are powerful words that can boost happiness and self-esteem.
- **Kindness and gratitude:** Kindness and gratitude are important social and emotional skills for children to master to feel happy and develop empathy.
- **Relaxation:** These activities promote relaxation through breath work, poses, and simple meditations. It is a curriculum for creating calmness, relaxation, and centering.

Throughout Part 2, mindfulness challenges, mindfulness variations, and brain challenges are included at the end of some of the activities. These challenges and variations can help you take the mindfulness activities a step further, based on your child's age and needs:

- **Mindfulness Challenges:** Brain growth is triggered by challenges, and each of your child's senses has its own structure and function in the brain. The more senses involved, the more exercise your child's brain is receiving. Mindfulness challenges are extra additions to the activity that require more focus, being present, and concentration.
- **Brain Challenges:** Science shows that when children face challenges and use information in new ways, it helps grow and strengthen the brain. Brain challenges require your child to use cognitive skills or problem-solving to figure out how to complete an activity or take the activity further. These challenges involve creativity and executive functioning skills.
- **Mindfulness Variations:** Researchers have found that when information is presented in a new way and children incorporate their senses, it contributes to new brain pathways. Mindfulness variations are a distinct or different way of doing a mindfulness activity. They may involve a partner, group, or adding a breathing exercise and/or movement to the activity.

Part 3, the final section of the book, provides advice for carrying a mindfulness practice into daily life and additional mindfulness strategies for you to teach your child.

Include Everyone

Anyone can learn mindfulness, including children with multiple special needs. All children are special and different in their own way. Don't worry if an exercise, pose, or movement includes something that is not possible for your child. If balancing on one leg is difficult, encourage her to use the wall to balance. You can modify the movement and explore different ways that work best for your child. Meet your child where he is and be attentive to how he responds to the different activities. Don't force activities that are uncomfortable.

Tips for Success

Before starting the activities in this book, here are a few pointers to have your kids keep in mind:

- **Noticing.** As you practice the activities in this book, it is important to have your children notice what is happening. Mindfulness is about noticing your physical sensations. Have them explore what they are feeling in their bodies before and after they try the activities. Did the experience change how they felt? Did it change their breathing or heart rate? A significant part of mindfulness is just noticing how you feel in the present moment.
- **Slow down.** To pay attention with your senses, it is important to do things slowly and with intention. When we rush through activities, we miss important details. Take your time with the activities in this book so your child can really notice what is happening in his or her body and mind.
- **Be barefoot if possible.** Being barefoot allows children to connect with the ground and find greater stability during the mindful movement poses and activities. Being barefoot allows children to stretch out their toes, which establishes a firmer foundation for balancing.
- **Do what feels right.** Your children should never feel pain while engaging in mindfulness activities. The key to children learning to be mindful is for them to be comfortable and have fun! If something doesn't feel right, don't force it. We want children to know that physical and mental fitness is enjoyable and an important process to help them feel calm, focused, and happy.
- **Be comfortable.** Provide a relaxing environment. Use yoga mats to make indoor surfaces more comfortable to sit on. Lower the lights and play soothing ambient

music (without words) to set the stage for mindfulness activities. It is also important to wear nonrestrictive, comfortable clothing. Children won't be fully present if they are bothered by bright lights, loud noises, or restrictive clothing.

- **Teach key terms and phrases.** Explain ahead of time what terms like "heart center," "starfish hands," "crown," and "roll your shoulders down your back" mean so that your child understands the instructions that mention those key terms. Also, you'll see that the scripts use words like "tail" instead of "buttocks" so kids don't get sidetracked with giggling.
- **Explain the benefits.** Children love to know the "why" behind the different activities. Teaching them about the brain, their senses, and how activities are helpful broadens their awareness of their own minds and behaviors. This helps children to better understand which daily mindfulness activities can help them when they are feeling moody, stressed, or just need to relax.
- **Post guidelines.** Have a set of guidelines for your child's mindfulness practice so that he or she knows what is expected. For example, "When the lights go off, so do our voices." "We are willing to try new activities." "We are kind to ourselves, others, and our environment." Guidelines set your child up for success and can influence his or her behavior.
- **Make a visual schedule.** Make a short visual schedule and post it on the wall so children know what's coming next. Try to have consistent directions at the beginning and end of your mindfulness practices. Routines build habits and help children feel secure.
- **Have fun.** Having an optimistic, happy attitude is contagious. Be playful and have fun with the activities. Don't be afraid to hiss like a snake or jump like a monkey. Model and engage in the activities with your child. Be patient, calm, and kind. Don't take the exercises too seriously; just enjoy yourself.

Mindfulness has a lot to offer children. The practices in this book will help your children become more connected to their mind, body, and feelings. With this increased connection, your children will develop awareness, which leads them to make better choices about how to react to themselves, others, and the environment. Let's get started.

PART TWO

Mindfulness Activities

Now that you have an understanding of what mindfulness is and what it can do for your child, you are ready to introduce the activities to your child. In this section, you will find information on mindful movement, mindful breathing, eating mindfully, positive affirmations, focus, kindness, gratitude, and relaxing. While all of the chapters are important, Mindful Breathing and Mindful Movement are essential to almost every activity in this section. Developing a habit of deep belly breathing helps calm and focus the mind so that mindful awareness can take place. All the activities are designed so that you can choose what resonates most with you and your child to build a happy practice that maximizes your child's potential. Together you will create a unique practice to manage stress, build resilience, and find inner peace!

CHAPTER 2

Mindful Movement

Believe it or not, mindful movement is essential to the learning process. Movement integrates new information and experiences into children's brains. Movement is essential to all the ways children express their learning, understanding, and themselves. When your child moves in an organized, graceful manner, his or her brain activates in a way that encourages learning. Mindful movement involves bringing awareness to the sensations in the body whether we are balancing, resting, or moving actively.

Mindful movement teaches children simple self-regulation strategies. Children begin to learn that they can control their breathing and heart rate, which leads to awareness of their brain-body relationship. Once they are aware of their bodies' signals, they are better able to handle their thoughts and feelings so that they can choose behaviors that are emotionally responsive.

This chapter begins with fundamental yoga poses that are used in the mindfulness practices that follow. However, yoga postures are just one way of mindfully moving. Any exercise that engages multiple senses, such as sight, smell, touch, hearing, movement, deep pressure, and taste, stimulates new pathways in the brain and is mindful. Use your imagination to find novel ways to move, as well—these movements will activate your child's senses and enhance brain activity and mindfulness.

Standing Poses

Standing poses build the foundation for mindfulness practices and for life. Standing poses use the body's large muscles, which promotes flexibility and strength. These poses focus on balance and grace, skills that, over time, can help boost children's confidence and self-esteem.

MOUNTAIN POSE

Mountain Pose is the foundation for many mindful standing poses and breathing activities. It teaches children how to achieve physical balance while they steady their minds. Children should return to Mountain Pose after other poses or breathing activities to center themselves before starting another activity.

Benefits

Mountain Pose is grounding—meaning that it connects children to the earth—and also centering—meaning that it helps them quiet their minds and focus on the present moment. Mountain Pose increases your child's body awareness and promotes good posture. The mindfulness variation of growing your mountain also stretches the front and sides of the body.

What to Say

- Stand up tall with your hands at your side. The palms of your hands should be facing forward. Let's wiggle our fingers to make sure they are relaxed. Plant your feet into the ground, but keep them relaxed. Don't grip with your toes. Let's wiggle our toes and spread them wide.
- Roll your shoulders up by your ears. Let them fall down your back. Squeeze your belly in. You are a tall, magnificent mountain!

Mindfulness Variation

Using the imagination will enhance this pose. Tell the children, "The mountains in Colorado are very tall. Pike's Peak is one of the tallest. Let's grow our mountains to be as tall as Pike's Peak. Stand up tall in Mountain Pose. Remember to relax your toes and fingers. Take a deep breath in as you raise your arms toward the sky. Bring your palms together to make the mountain peak. Look up at your hands. Is there snow on your peak?"

WARRIOR I POSE

Warrior I Pose is part of a series of yoga poses that focuses on building strength. When children and teens hold these poses and practice deep breathing, it teaches them how to be strong and deal with stress.

Benefits

Warrior I Pose strengthens your child's legs, upper back, and shoulders. It is a good stretch for the hips and calves. It also builds children's inner strength and determination.

What to Say

- Begin in Mountain Pose. Take a big step back with your left foot. Bend your front knee. Straighten your back leg. Keep your hips facing forward. Stand up tall and raise your arms up to the sky, with your palms facing each other.
- Be a peaceful warrior by letting your shoulders fall down your back while keeping your arms in the air. Say, "I am powerful."
- Move back to Mountain Pose. Let's switch legs and do the other side.

WARRIOR II POSE

In yoga, Warrior II Pose is a popular transitional pose because it is the foundation for several other poses. It helps the body flow from pose to pose.

Benefits

Warrior II Pose makes your child's entire body feel strong. It is also a gentle hip stretch. Warrior II Pose builds mental strength and resiliency.

What to Say

- Begin in Mountain Pose. Take a big step back with your right foot. Your front foot is pointing forward and your back foot is pointed toward the side of your mat.
- Bend your front knee, but make sure you can still see your big toe. Turn your hips to the long edge of your mat.
- Reach your arms straight out in opposite directions. Say, "I am strong." Look over your front fingertips. What a fierce Warrior II! Now let's do the other side.

Seated Poses

Seated poses enhance flexibility in children's hips, which can become tight from too much sitting. They also help children feel strong, grounded, and focused as they engage in mindfulness activities.

EASY SEATED POSE

Easy Seated Pose is a foundational yoga pose that is great for practicing breathing exercises, mindfulness, or meditating. Even though the name implies it is easy, it can be quite difficult to remain in this position for long periods of time, especially if you are little and full of wiggles.

Benefits

Easy Seated Pose encourages good posture and is calming. It creates balance and grounding. Sitting up tall enhances concentration, focus, and mindful awareness.

What to Say

- Sit with your legs crossed. Slump forward and try to take a deep breath in through your nose. What did you notice?
- Now let's sit tall with our legs crossed. Place your hands on your knees. Sit up a little taller. Breathe in. Roll your shoulders up by your ears. Breathe out, and let your shoulders fall down your back. Take a few breaths. What did you notice this time?

WASHER POSE

Washer Pose is a fun twisting pose from Kundalini yoga. The "psssh" washing-machine sound that your child makes teaches him about breath control.

Benefits

This pose stimulates internal organs and helps with digestion. It also improves posture. The twisting engages the vestibular sensory system (this system provides your body with information about balance and spatial awareness—we will explore sensory systems more in Chapter 4).

What to Say

- Sit up tall in Easy Seated Pose. Bring your hands to your shoulders with elbows out. Take a deep breath in.
- Twist slowly from side to side while breathing, making a "psssh, psssh, psssh" sound.
- Come back to Easy Seated Pose. Notice how you feel. Do you have more energy or less energy?

ROCK 'N' ROLL POSE

Rock 'n' Roll Pose is a fun way to transition from lying on your back to Easy Seated Pose or any seated position. It is also a gentle wake-up pose for little ones.

Benefits

Rock 'n' Roll Pose massages and increases flexibility in your child's spine. The rocking motion has a soothing, relaxing effect.

What to Say

- We are going to rock 'n' roll! Lie on your back. Bend your knees and hug them to your heart.
- Close your eyes. Begin to rock from side to side. Take a mindful breath in. What do you notice? Now rock back and forth. Keep rocking until you feel calm and relaxed.
- Rock up to Easy Seated Pose. Take four slow, mindful breaths. Open your eyes. How do you feel?

Balancing Poses

Balancing poses improve focus and teach resilience. Practicing balancing helps children strengthen their brain-body awareness and develop self-regulation skills. Balancing poses require a nonmoving focal point. It can be anything that remains still, from a water bottle to a picture on the wall.

TREE POSE

Tree Pose is a fun and easy pose that builds focus. The ancient yogis believed that being able to hold Tree Pose with ease reflects a balanced emotional state.

Benefits

This popular pose enhances children's focus and concentration. It improves their balance and posture while increasing flexibility and strength.

What to Say

- Trees are strong and beautiful. Let's be trees! Begin in Mountain Pose. Plant your entire right foot into the mat. Shift your weight to your right foot. Place the ball of your left foot and your left heel on the inside of your right leg above or below your knee. Placing the foot on your knee can cause damage to your knee over time. Look down. You should have made a triangle with your legs!
- Bring your hands together at your heart center. Find something that is not moving to gaze at. This helps you to balance.
- Once you feel steady, grow your branches to the sky. Challenge yourself by looking up or closing your eyes. What do you notice? Are you a steady tree or are your branches a little wobbly? Take a deep breath in. Let it go.
- Shake your foot out and become a tree on your other leg. Notice how you feel on this side. Is it different from the first tree? Don't forget to breathe.

Mindfulness Challenge

Tell the children, "Find a partner. Stand side by side, and wrap one arm around your partner's shoulders. Make a triangle with your outer legs by placing them below your knees to form Tree Pose. With your partner, hop from one side of the room to the other. If one of you loses the pose, pause for a moment and then try again."

AIRPLANE POSE

Airplane Pose builds strength and balance. It is part of the Warrior series and in adult yoga it is called Warrior III. This fun pose can result in a lot of airplanes crashing. Therefore young children may want to use a wall for support until they are confident and have found their balance.

Benefits

Airplane Pose strengthens the back, core, and glutes. It stretches the hamstrings and improves focus and concentration. Children practice to control their physical and emotional responses to remain balanced.

What to Say

- We are going to be airplanes. Stand up tall in Mountain Pose with your hands at your heart. Take a mindful breath in.
- Prepare to fly by first noticing your feet. Wiggle your toes and spread them wide. Breathe out slowly. Notice how it feels to shift your weight to your right foot.
- Mindfully and slowly kick your left leg back as you start to tip forward. Find a place on the floor to focus your eyes on. Lift off and balance. Touch a nearby wall for support if you need to. When you feel balanced, spread your arms out like wings. Soar higher! Slowly come back to Mountain Pose. Shake it out. We have one more side to do!

DANCER POSE

Dancer is a pose with many steps, which means it is good for building working memory and cognitive skills. Dancer Pose may need to be practiced near a wall or modified to just standing up tall with one foot held in a hand before attempting to reach forward and kick the foot into the hand.

Benefits

Dancer Pose improves your child's posture, balance, and focus. It stretches hips, legs, and shoulders and strengthens the upper and lower back, legs, and shoulders.

What to Say

- Stand up tall in Mountain Pose. We are going to be graceful dancers! Reach your right arm up toward the sky. Hold the other arm out as if you are holding a serving tray. Pretend your left elbow is glued to your side.
- Bring your weight on to your right foot. Bend your left knee and reach back with your left hand to grab the inside arch of your foot.
- Take a deep breath in, find a focus point, and stand up tall. Once you feel balanced, start to reach forward as you kick your foot into your hand. Great! Now switch sides.

Brain Challenge

For groups of children ages nine and older, instruct them to work together to do a group Dancer Pose with their hands all meeting in the middle of a circle. Making a group Dancer Pose will enhance executive functioning skills and teamwork.

Backbends

Backbends energize the body and open the shoulders and heart. They also work to counteract the effects of any activities that lead to shallow breathing, such as sitting, screen time, and stress. Practice backbends when you and your child are in the need of an energy boost.

COBRA POSE

Children love to slither on the floor and pretend to be snakes, but being a cobra has multiple, specific benefits. Cobra Pose integrates the Tonic Labyrinthine Reflex (TLR), which is a primitive foundational brainstem reflex present in newborns that supports the integration of other reflexes. Cobra Pose is related to the prone TLR, the reflex present when babies and children are lying on their stomachs. The TLR provides the baby's first response to gravity. The prone TLR happens when a child lies on her stomach and gravity causes her head, arms, and legs to be pulled down toward the ground. When the baby feels that, her body will curl inward with her chin tucked and knees tucking under her stomach. The TLR links the vestibular system to the proprioceptive system and helps control the body's muscle tone via regulating flexion/extension so that the initial response doesn't become fixed. If primitive reflexes are not integrated, they can lead to developmental delays, sensory processing problems, and learning problems. Because of its therapeutic benefits, Cobra Pose is a great activity for children of all ages and abilities.

Benefits

Slithering around on the floor builds upper-body strength and coordination. Vocalizing a long "hisss" releases tension and coordinates breath with movement. Cobra Pose's connection to the TLR helps children reach developmental milestones. Cobra Pose also tones the nerves by strengthening the spine and improving communication between the brain and the body. It also opens the chest and lungs and stimulates appetite.

What to Say

- Let's be strong cobras playing in the grass! Lie on your belly with your legs glued together. Put your hands under your shoulders. Breathe in deeply as you lift your head and chest.

- Let out a long "hisss." Raise your hands slightly and let them hover in place off the mat. Cobras don't have hands. Keep your lower body, from your belly to your toes, glued to the floor as you lift up. Remember to make your tail long and straight by pointing your toes.
- Lower yourself down to rest in the grass.
- Try it again. This time move your head from side to side as you hiss.
- Try it a third time. This time slither forward using only your hands and arms to move (this works best on slippery flooring).

Mindfulness Variation

Tell the children, "Your cobra has an itchy head. If your cobra wants to scratch his head he has to use the end of his tail (your toes). Raise yourself up to Cobra Pose, but widen your knees and arch your back a little more. Raise your feet toward your head. Scratch all the itchy spots with your toes. Then lower down into the grass. Take a few deep breaths to relax after the backbend."

LOCUST POSE

Locusts are grasshoppers with long legs that help them launch high into the air. Locust Pose is a powerful backbend that requires a little practice, so it might take some time to achieve.

Benefits

Locust Pose makes children feel strong and powerful. It strengthens the back and the legs. Locust Pose also lengthens the spine and stretches the arms and legs.

What to Say

- Lie on your belly with your forehead resting on the ground. Pretend that your legs are glued together and keep your arms close to your sides. Make your body like one long board.
- Take a deep breath in. Slowly lift your arms, legs, and head off the ground. Look forward. Remember to keep everything glued together. Take in one more breath. Lift a little higher. Let your breath go and relax down to the ground. That was fun! Let's try it one more time.

CAMEL POSE

Camel Pose is a favorite in children's yoga classes! This pose gets its name because when your child bends backward, his body will resemble a camel's hump. Camel Pose opens the chest, which helps your child to relax and de-stress.

Benefits

Camel Pose opens the chest, which increases lung capacity. This is great for children with asthma and respiratory issues. It also improves your child's posture, which is beneficial for droopy shoulders and rounded backs.

What to Say

- Did you know that camels store fat, not water, in their humps? Let's be camels and make that hump. We are going to make the hump with our hearts by opening them toward the ceiling!
- Kneel on the floor with your knees two fists apart. Push the tops of your feet into the floor. Make your hands into fists and bring them to your lower back. Pull your belly in to engage your tummy muscles.
- Open through your heart center by bringing your elbows together behind your back. Continue to lift your heart with each mindful breath, letting your head gently fall back as far as is comfortable. If you can, bring your hands to your heels to make the camel's hump. Take a deep breath in. Let it go.
- Come to a sitting position on your feet with your hands on your lap. Close your eyes. What do you notice?

FISH POSE

Fish Pose is a graceful, but powerful backbend that can give relief to symptoms of asthma and bronchitis. Young children or children with special needs may find Fish Pose challenging to get into, but it can be easily modified by having them lie on a small child bolster, rolled-up mat, or blanket to provide the same benefits. Modifying Fish Pose is called Supported Fish. It can be a relaxing pose that counteracts the effects of too much screen time.

Benefits

The gentle bend of the chest mimics the rounded back of a fish. The opening of the chest releases feelings of positivity and well-being. Fish Pose reduces chest disorders and promotes a healthy heart. This pose can also stimulate the thyroid, which increases metabolism.

What to Say

- We are going to be a fish! Lie on your back. Straighten your legs and glue them together. Slide your hands under your bottom. Bring them close together with palms facing down.
- As you breathe in, push your elbows down. Point your toes. Tilt your head back until the top of it touches the floor. You are a fish! Take five deep breaths. Slowly release to the floor. Hugging your hands around the knees or under the knees, bring them into your heart center. Rock and roll a few times side to side. Ah...feels good!

Mindful Brain-Building Moves

Cross-lateral movements involve arms and legs crossing over the body's midline. The left side of the brain controls the right side of the body, and the right side of the brain controls the left side. When arms and legs cross the body's midline, the two sides communicate. This integration of both sides of the brain enhances learning. This section contains fun cross-lateral moves that should be part of every child's mindfulness practice.

CROSS CRAWLS

This exercise is similar to walking in place, but with a twist. The Cross Crawl is a good movement for a "brain break" to prepare your child for activities that require focus.

Benefits

The alternating right and left hands touching the opposite knees activate the left and right sides of the brain and body simultaneously. It also connects the upper and lower halves of the body. By combining movement and touch, this exercise stimulates both the motor and sensory regions of the brain, and increases communication between the left and right hemispheres of the brain.

What to Say

- Stand tall in Mountain Pose. We are going to hike through some tall jungle grass. Let's start by lifting one arm and the opposite leg. Now lift the other leg and arm and start to walk in place.
- The grass is so tall in the jungle! It's hard to see where we are going. We need to push the grass out of the way by bringing our arm across our body and tapping the opposite knee.
- Keep going very slowly. We don't know what is lurking in this tall jungle grass. Reach across your body each time.
- Mindfully listen. What do you hear? I think we need to move faster. Let's pick up the pace, adding a bounce to each step.
- Now come back to Mountain Pose. Close your eyes. Take a few deep breaths. What do you notice?

CATERPILLAR CRAWL

The Caterpillar Crawl is a group activity that incorporates crawling, which is important for your child's brain and body development even after she has learned to walk. The Caterpillar Crawl is a great way to get information flowing between the two hemispheres of the brain while having fun.

Benefits

Crawling is a form of "heavy work," which helps to organize and calm the nervous system, especially when combined with deep breathing. Cross-lateral movements activate both sides of the brain and enhance learning. Crawling also helps hand strength and motor skills by separating the two sides of each hand. Yes, there are actually two sides to the hand (the fourth and fifth fingers are a unit, and the thumb, index, and third finger are the other side). Being able to use both sides separately is fundamental to using scissors, buttons, and writing instruments. The Caterpillar Crawl also enhances balance, core strength, body awareness, coordination, and motor planning.

What to Say

- We are going to mindfully crawl like a caterpillar does. Let's form a line with everyone on their hands and knees.
- Gently grasp the ankles of the child in front of you. We are now a long caterpillar.
- Take a deep breath in. What do you notice? Let's start to slowly and mindfully move as a caterpillar around the room. What do you see as a caterpillar? What do you hear?
- Okay, caterpillar, stop moving. Release your grip on your friend's ankles and come up to a seated position. Tell me what you noticed while you were crawling.

DEAD BUG

The Dead Bug activity mimics the body position of a dead bug. It's a great wake-up exercise to do with your kids following relaxation time. (It's an easy transition since children are probably already lying on their backs.) And let's be honest—lying on the floor waving your limbs in the air never gets old. It is a great way to de-stress children of all ages. Try it for yourself.

Benefits

Dead Bug calms and restores the central nervous system and strengthens the core. Plus, making "Xs" in the air with the legs and arms is a locomotor movement, which crosses the brain's and body's midlines, helping to balance and organize the brain's hemispheres.

What to Say

- Lie on your back. Lift up your arms and legs. Lengthen your arms and legs to build core strength.
- Breathe in and out while floating your arms slowly back and forth, making "Xs" in the air.

Mindfulness Variation

Dead Bug can also be done as a partner pose with toddlers. Parents, lie on your back. Bend your knees, keep your shins together, and place your child on his stomach on your lower legs between your knees and your ankles. Hold his hands and sway your feet back and forth slowly. Remember to breathe in and out as you move.

YOGA BICYCLES

Yoga Bicycles involve children lying on their backs, pretending to ride a bicycle. This activity is a good exercise for children of all ages, easy to incorporate into little yoga stories, and can be used as a brain break when studying.

Benefits

Yoga Bicycles strengthen the core and upper back muscles. The activity also enhances awareness of the core muscles and is centering and grounding to children. Yoga Bicycles also aid in digestion and are a brain-building exercise because bilateral coordination integrates the right and left hemispheres of the brain.

What to Say

- We are going on a mindful bike ride. Lie on your back. Bring your hands in front of your face and interlace your fingers to form a helmet. Now place your fingers/helmet behind and under your neck. Spread your elbows out wide.
- Bend your knees and lift your legs. As you breathe in, lift your head and shoulders off the ground. Relax your shoulders, reach one elbow toward its opposite, lifted knee, and straighten the other leg.
- Let all your breath out. Take a breath in. Slowly return to center. Let your breath out as you twist to the other side.
- Bring your awareness to your tummy muscles and imagine you have an "X" traced on your body from your tummy to your shoulders. This exercise is making the "X" stronger. Notice which muscles you are using. Are you straining your neck or head? If so, take a break, breathe deeply, and then begin again.

"Hello, Sunshine"

"Hello, Sunshine" is a yoga sequence that flows from pose to pose. It is traditionally called a Sun Salutation, since it is a series of poses that are meant to greet the sun after you wake up in the morning. "Hello, Sunshine" is a great way to wake up your child's brain and body for a day of learning. First we will individually introduce the poses, then we will put them all together for a flow.

FORWARD FOLD

Forward Fold is a calming pose; however, it can be a bit challenging, especially if your child has tight hamstrings. Children sometimes need a little inspiration to stay in this pose so make it fun by having them count their toes or tickle a stuffed animal.

Benefits

Forward Fold calms the central nervous system and relieves fatigue. It stretches the hamstrings and the backside of the body. It helps with digestion and concentration.

What to Say

- Start in Mountain Pose with your feet two fists apart. Take a deep breath in through your nose as you reach your arms toward the sky. Bring your palms together.
- Let your breath go as you bring your hands down the center line of your body to your toes. Fold your body at the waist.
- Keep a slight bend in your knees and let your head hang heavy. Nod your head "yes" and shake your head "no" to relieve any tightness. Let your arms be loose and relaxed.

MONKEY POSE

Sometimes our thoughts are like monkeys, jumping around and having a hard time settling down. Kids already love pretending to be monkeys—help them add a mindful breath to the fun, and find a moment of stillness! There are many variations on Monkey Pose—this one is also sometimes called a Half Sun Salute.

Benefits

Monkey jumps build strength in the legs. Monkey Pose is a good stretch for tight legs. This exercise also teaches children how to calm their minds with their breath.

What to Say

- From Forward Fold, bring your hands up right below the knees, and place your palms on your shins.
- Take a deep breath in and stretch your spine out long. As you let your breath out, make monkey sounds. Jump up and down a few times.
- Come back to a still monkey. Take one more breath in. Slowly let it out. Take one more breath in, notice the stillness. As you let your breath out, fold forward again.

DOWN DOG POSE

Down Dog Pose resembles a dog stretching after a long nap. It is a popular children's pose that provides a good stretch, while allowing children to have fun barking, walking, and pretending to be dogs.

Benefits

Down Dog Pose strengthens the back, arms, and shoulders. It also relieves stiffness in the shoulders and stretches the hamstrings and calves. Best of all, it's calming and it feels good.

What to Say

- Start on your mat on all fours. Spread your fingers wide like a doggy paw. Press your doggy paws into the mat.
- Tuck your toes and push your tail (or hips) high into the air so that your legs are straight and your heels are pushing into the mat. Let your head hang heavy. Make doggy sounds!

Mindfulness Variation

Say to the children, "We are happy dogs because we love going on a walk! Wag your tail back and forth slowly. Let's start walking. Bend one knee and then the other. Keep your doggy paws (hands) planted. Dogs like to mark their territory on walks. I see a fire hydrant. Raise your right leg up and open your hips to the right. Keep pressing through your doggy paws with only a slight bend in your arms. Look under your right arm. Breathe mindfully in and out through the nose. Repeat on the other side. That was a long walk. Roll onto your back for a belly rub and rest. Put your doggy paws in the air. Maybe scratch behind your ears. Take a few deep breaths."

PLANK POSE

Planks are strong, sturdy pieces of wood extending from ships. In pirate movies, you might see that planks can hold even the biggest of pirates. In yoga, Plank Pose is a transition pose from standing poses to poses that require children to lie on their mats.

Benefits

Plank Pose is a strengthening pose for the legs, abdomen, and upper body. It promotes good posture and enhances body awareness and confidence.

What to Say

- Start on all fours on your mat. Spread your fingers wide like a starfish. Curl your toes under and lift your knees off the ground. Keep your arms straight and strong.
- Try to make your body straight and long, like a piece of wood. You should be looking at the floor, but keep your head in line with your body. Don't let your head droop.
- Pull your belly muscles in. Take a deep breath in. Feel your body getting stronger. Let your breath out.
- Lower all the way to the floor. Turn your head to one side and take a few deep mindful breaths, noticing the sensations in your body.

"HELLO, SUNSHINE" SEQUENCE

Benefits

"Hello, Sunshine" has multiple benefits for children. Sun Salutations limber up and energize the body, especially the back, making it flexible and strong. Sun Salutations improve focus and concentration by teaching children to link their breath with movement. Additionally, this "Hello, Sunshine" stretch improves working memory, clears the mind, and brings a smile to your face.

What to Say

- Start in Mountain Pose with your feet firmly planted two fists length apart. Hold your hands together at your heart center. Take a big breath in and let it out. Imagine yourself as a strong mountain, standing tall, with your feet planted.

- As you take a deep breath in, grow your mountain by stretching your arms up high above your head. Keep your hands together to make the mountain peak.
- As you breathe out, keep palms together as you slowly fold forward, bending your knees. Bring your hands to the ground in front of you, keeping your palms flat. Shake your head "no" and nod your head "yes."
- Come up halfway into Monkey Pose. Bring your hands back to the ground in front of you. Your knees should be bent. Plant your hands.
- Step one leg back as far as you can, and then the other. Push back through your heels, keeping your legs straight. Imagine that your whole body is stiff and strong like a plank of wood. It's okay to drop to your knees. Say, "I am strong."
- Slowly lower all the way to the floor. Take a big breath in and lift your head and heart up as you hiss a long breath out. This is Cobra Pose, which we discussed before.
- Push slowly back up to Plank Pose (knees up or down). Tuck your toes under and lift your tail high for Down Dog Pose. Hold here for a few breaths. Wag your tail or walk your dog.
- As you exhale, look forward at your hands, bend your knees, and hop or walk both feet forward toward your hands and squat down like a frog. Then raise your tail up for Forward Fold.
- Take a deep breath in as you come up halfway for Monkey Pose. Bring your hands back to the ground in front of you. Keep your knees bent. Breathe out as you plant your hands.
- Take a deep breath in as you straighten your legs and sweep your arms wide as you stand with hands above your head with palms together. Grow tall, mountain! Exhale as you bring your hands down to your heart center.
- Take a deep breath in. As you let it out, say, "Hello, sunshine!" This completes the "Hello, Sunshine" sequence. Let's do it again!

Resting Poses

Resting poses enhance feelings of peace, calm, and relaxation in children. In yoga or mindfulness activities, resting poses are usually done after the work or toward the end of a class. Resting poses encourage a quiet mind and provide a time to focus on the breath.

STARFISH

Starfish is a great pose to introduce small children to relaxation. Children love pretending to be still as a starfish as they wait for the waves to roll over them. This exercise is good to do at the end of a yoga class or right before going to bed.

Materials

- Exercise ball (or other similar ball like a beach ball or softball)

Benefits

The deep pressure of the exercise ball coupled with deep breathing is calming to children. Lying still like a starfish helps children settle their minds and bodies so they feel peaceful and relaxed.

What to Say

- Lie down on your back. Spread your arms and legs out wide. Close your eyes.
- Imagine you are a starfish resting on the beach. If you lie mindfully, you may feel the waves roll over you and then move back out to sea. (Take an exercise ball, apply a little pressure, and roll it over your child's body, front and back, as he lies quietly breathing.)
- With your next breath in, fill your belly with air. Imagine that your starfish grows bigger as you breathe in and then smaller as you breathe out. Keep breathing while feeling the waves wash over you. Notice how you feel.

MUMMY POSE

A mummy is a body that is wrapped up and not moving. It lies very still with its arms crossed. Children find lying still a challenge, so making Mummy Pose a multisensory experience will help them to rest longer.

Benefits

Mummy Pose relaxes the mind, reduces fatigue, and builds awareness of the brain and body.

What to Say

- We are going to pretend to be a mummy. Lie on your back with your arms across your heart, making an "X."
- Close your eyes. What do you notice? Take a deep breath in. Let all the air go. Continue to breathe deeply.
- Slowly rise to Easy Seated Pose. Notice how you feel.

Mindfulness Variation

To make this a multisensory experience, consider introducing other elements: add an eye pillow filled with lavender or treated with lavender essential oil, hold the child's ankles while gently rocking him or her from side to side, or play ambient music (with no words).

CHILD'S POSE

Child's Pose can also be called Baby Pose or Acorn, but most call it Child's Pose, since it looks like a baby or child sleeping. It is very calming and helps center children when they are having a bad day. Best of all, it can be done anywhere.

Benefits

Anytime you bend your body in half at the hips, you are doing a Forward Fold. Bending forward is calming to the nervous system and relieves stress. Child's Pose can ease back strain and it stretches the arms. Child's Pose centers and grounds children, which reduces excess energy.

What to Say

- Sit on your feet. Your knees can be together or open wide. Rest your forehead on the ground. Your arms can rest beside you with palms facing up or you can reach toward the top of the mat with palms facing down.
- Close your eyes and allow your body to relax.
- Breathe in and out slowly through the nose. Notice where you feel your breath. Is it in your belly? Your back? Or both?
- Slowly and gently rise to a seated position. Notice how you feel.

Mindfulness Variation

If your child is having a tough day, this extra dose of calm can be just the trick to reset his mood. Have your child move into Child's Pose. Sit behind him and firmly run the palms of your hands up and down his back from top to bottom. This will stretch and open the vertebrae in the spine. Rest your hands one on top of the other at the base of his spine. (At the base of the spine just above the sacrum, there is an area where several nerve endings come together. When you apply gentle pressure to this area it has a calming effect on the nervous system.) Together, take a mindful breath in. As you release your breath, apply slight pressure to your child's back with your hands. Breathe with him for ten breaths. If your child is still upset, take more breaths. While breathing, visualize calm, positive energy coming out of your hands. Draw your hands firmly up and down your child's back one more time, then release them. Take in a couple of mindful breaths while sitting in Easy Seated Pose. Resume your routine. This variation can be done several times if needed.

Mindful Movement in Nature

When you do movement exercises outside, you offer your child all the benefits of physical activity plus the mentally rejuvenating benefits of being in nature. In addition, being outside is wonderful for mindfulness because there's always a sound, sight, smell, or texture to focus on.

BIKE RIDING

Riding a bike on an easy trail will help children feel calm and peaceful, making it easier to listen to the sounds of nature, feel the wind, and be fully present. This is an experience the entire family can share!

Benefits

Research is beginning to show us that this multisensory activity can improve executive functioning tasks, such as working memory, flexibility, and self-control. Research has also shown that children who ride a bike report feeling more positive and emotionally centered after riding.

What to Say

- We are going to ride our bikes mindfully, paying attention with all our senses to what is happening around us.
- Notice what you see, hear, feel, and smell. Let's go!
- Now that we're done, does everyone want to tell the group about one interesting sight or smell they noticed? Did you feel different after your ride?

TAI CHI

Tai Chi is an exercise that originated in China for self-defense. It is a series of self-paced movements that are completed in a slow, mindful manner. Each movement is coordinated with breathing and flows into the next without stopping. This exercise is a way to introduce children to Tai Chi.

Benefits

Tai Chi helps children relax, focus, and find inner peace. The animal and nature visualizations make it engaging to children, allowing them to let go of anger and stress.

What to Say

- We are going to make a ball of energy. This ball of energy comes from an exercise program called Tai Chi.
- Stand up tall in Mountain Pose. Take a slow, deep breath in. Let it go. Rub your hands together very quickly, the same way you might rub them on a cold day. Notice the feeling in your hands as you rub them together. Are they warm or cold?
- Now, keeping your palms touching, stop rubbing your hands. What do you feel? Can you feel the energy in your hands? Do you feel the warmth and connection between your hands?
- Slowly move them apart. Keep your fingers relaxed and move smoothly. When you start to feel the pull between your hands become weak, bring them closer to each other. Repeat this process. Slowly move your hands apart and then back together. Maintain a smooth pace. Can you feel the energy in your hands? What does it feel like?

MINDFUL WALKING

Mindful Walking simply means walking with mindful awareness. Your child will bring her attention to her breath and feet. Mindful Walking can be done anywhere, but it is best practiced outside and barefoot. During Mindful Walking, children should walk in a slow, relaxed manner, noticing sounds, feelings, and smells.

Benefits

Mindful Walking enhances body and mindful awareness. Children will focus on things that are usually taken for granted, like their feet. Mindful Walking improves concentration, attention, and focus.

What to Say

- Take your shoes and socks off and stand up tall in Mountain Pose.
- Be tall and strong, but relaxed and comfortable. Notice how your feet feel on the ground. Try shifting your weight from one side to the other to see how it feels. Lean side to side, forward, and backward.
- Let's go for a walk. Start to notice how your feet feel as you walk. What do you feel in your heels? In your toes? After a few moments, start to notice what walking feels like in your body. What happens to your arms as you walk? Can you feel it in your face?
- If your mind starts to wander, gently bring it back and start to notice how your body is feeling during the walk. Stop in Mountain Pose. Take a big breath in and sigh it out.

MINDFUL JUNGLE COURSE

Mindful Jungle Course is an obstacle course with a jungle theme. Children love to jump, run, roll, and crawl—especially if there is a jungle theme involved. Get creative! Use Bubble Wrap, tunnels, beanbags, and whatever else you can find to make this a course that incorporates all the senses.

Materials

- Yoga blocks, stepping stones, or small mats

Benefits

Moving through an obstacle strengthens motor planning skills. Obstacle courses encourage focus, concentration, and attention skills. Additionally, your child is building muscle strength and coordination.

What to Say

- Let's take off our shoes so we can feel every movement our feet make.
- Imagine you are an animal in the jungle, moving from rock to tree to bush. Try not to touch the floor. Move slowly, feeling your feet. Notice how your weight shifts as you hop over crocodiles and balance on stepping stones.
- Move through the jungle course three to five times, paying attention to how you move.

CHAPTER 3

Mindful Breathing

Breathing is one of the most important things we do, alongside eating. And like eating, breathing provides our bodies with energy. The ancient yogis believed the breath is a bridge between the mind and body. When we control our breath, in a certain way, to produce a specific feeling, we are practicing pranayama. *Pranayama* is the term given to breathing practice in yoga and mindfulness. There are many different types of pranayama in children's mindfulness. Some mindful breathing practices help children focus and be more energized, while others help children quiet their minds.

Once your child begins to practice mindful breathing regularly, he will experience the amazing effects it has on his well-being. When practiced correctly, mindful breathing can reduce stress and teach children how to relax, manage frustrations, and be resilient.

But let's be honest: sitting quietly and practicing breathing exercises can be hard for children. So how can you make breathing fun? The exercises in this chapter will teach you how to incorporate language that resonates with kids, include the senses, use props, and make breathing part of a story or obstacle course. When children recognize they are in control of their bodies, through their breath, they can reduce stress, improve focus, and enhance their happiness anytime, anywhere.

Energizing Breathing Exercises

Though people joke that kids always have too much energy, sometimes they do need a nudge to get them going in the morning or in a late-afternoon slump. These breathing execises will help them perk up—without sugar!

VOLCANO BREATH

Volcano Breath is a quick and easy breathing technique that is coupled with movement to release anger, stress, or tension. Exploding our hands to our sides engages one of our hidden senses, proprioception (a body/spatial awareness sense), which is activated when we contract and stretch our muscles. This hidden sense helps children feel calm.

Benefits

Volcano Breath helps children understand visualization. Inner imagery is a powerful tool to create positive change. When you imagine the anger or stress exploding out, it helps to move the emotion. Volcano Breath also enhances bilateral coordination and is fun, empowering, and centering to children.

What to Say

- Volcano Breath is a way to feel in control and happier.
- We are going to begin standing in Mountain Pose with feet slightly apart. Bring your hands to your heart center with palms together—we call this Namaste Hands.
- Breathe in slowly through your nose as you bring your hands above your head. Pause with your arms above your head. Breathe out through your nose as you separate your hands.
- Just like a volcano exploding forcefully, move your arms down to each side. Let your palms hit your thighs.
- Repeat three more times. Notice how you feel.

"LET IT GO" BREATH

"Let It Go" Breath is a breathing exercise that helps children release tension, stress, or any other emotions they want to move past. When breathing is combined with bowing the head, it enhances the centering effects of the breathing exercise.

Benefits

"Let It Go" Breath is fun, and it releases stress, provides energy, and lightens the mood. Folding forward has a calming effect on the brain and nervous system. Reaching and stretching upward lengthens the spine and is energizing.

What to Say

- "Let It Go" Breath is a way to let go of something that's bothering you.
- Stand up tall in Mountain Pose. Take a big step sideways with one foot. Turn your toes slightly in. Think of something that bothered you that you keep thinking about again and again.
- Bring your arms up over your head as you take in a big breath through your nose. Breathe in a little more as you reach up for the sky. Let your breath go in a long "haaa."
- As you fold forward, let your arms fall between your legs. Let all your worries and thoughts go as you breathe out. Repeat ten times. How do you feel now?

LION'S BREATH

Lion's Breath is a breathing technique that goes with Lion's Pose in yoga. It is a powerful breathing method that uses a forceful exhale. The name refers to the lionlike expression on the child's face and the roaring sound that the breath makes when exhaled.

Benefits

Lion's Breath, when coupled with Lion's Pose, provides sensory awareness in the form of proprioception, which helps improve focus. This fun breathing technique releases excess energy and relieves tension in the body.

What to Say

- We are going to breathe like lions. Ready?
- Start by sitting like a lion. Sit on your feet with big toes together and knees opened wide. Spread your fingers like a starfish.
- Sit up tall. Take a deep breath in through your nose. Open your mouth and stick your tongue out as your body moves forward onto your hands. Forcefully push your weight into your hands like a lion pouncing out of the forest.
- Be a peaceful lion with a powerful pounce by rocking forward so that your hands land on the ground. Let's add a whisper roar by opening our mouths, moving our tongues forward, and making a "haaa" sound as we breathe out. Repeat ten times.

BUNNY BREATH

Bunny Breath is the kid-friendly version of the traditional "breath of fire" in Kundalini yoga. Breath of fire is a powerful breathing exercise that uses rapid breathing to move energy and increase blood circulation. So as not to overdo it, children can do a modified version of this exercise, taking only three small sniffs.

Benefits

If your child is feeling kind of blah, Bunny Breath will provide plenty of energy, focus, and a clear mind. Breathing exercises produce a strong respiratory system, improved posture, and happiness.

What to Say

- Let's be bunnies! But before we begin, sit up tall, close your eyes, and notice how you feel. Sit up tall on your heels like a bunny sitting in the grass.
- Take three quick sniffs in through the nose. Pause. Now breathe out through your mouth slowly in a sigh.
- Repeat four times. How do you feel? Is it different from before you pretended to be a bunny?

WAKE-UP BREATH

Do your kids ever have days where it is just hard for them to wake up, or they wake up on the wrong side of the bed? These are the mornings for Wake-Up Breath. Wake-Up Breath energizes the face, neck, and shoulders and refreshes our energy for a day of learning.

Benefits

Wake-Up Breath is an energizing breathing exercise that not only helps children find some energy when they are feeling fatigued, but also releases tension and tightness in the face, shoulders, and neck.

What to Say

- Let's start our day off right by waking up our face and shoulders with our breath. Sit up tall in Easy Seated Pose. Take a deep, slow breath in through your nose. Let it out through your nose too.
- Take another breath in. Pause. Open your eyes wide. Blink. Let your breath out through your nose.
- Take a breath in. Pause. Move your eyebrows up and down. Let your breath out slowly.
- Take a breath in. Pause. Open your mouth wide and move your jaw back and forth. Let your breath out.
- Take a deep breath in. Pause. Wrinkle your face up. Really scrunch it up. Relax and let your breath out.
- Take a breath in. Pause. Roll your neck in one direction, then the other direction. Let your breath out slowly.
- Deep breath in. Bring your shoulders up by your ears. Let your breath out as you let your shoulders drop. Repeat four times.
- Sit up tall as you take a deep breath in. Let it all the way out. How do you feel?

Calming Breathing Exercises

All kids need to rein in their energy at one point or another. Instead of plopping them in front of a screen, try a breathing exercise to shift from a high-energy activity to a quiet one.

BALLOON BREATH

Balloon Breath is a great way to introduce children to deep, diaphragmatic breathing. It is a slow-paced exercise that produces a state of calm. Balloon Breath focuses on matching the length of the breath in to the length of the breath out. It is a good breathing exercise to use to begin and end a mindfulness practice.

Benefits

Balloon Breath relieves frustration and decreases excessive energy. It teaches children how to breathe from their diaphragm, which reduces anxiety and stress. It also reduces heart rate and blood pressure and draws awareness inward, which helps with focus.

What to Say

- Let's make some balloons with our breath.
- Sit or stand up tall. The taller you stand or sit, the better you breathe. The better you breathe, the better you feel.
- Roll your shoulders back and down.
- Breathe in through your nose as you sweep your hands wide, making a big balloon.
- Fill your belly up with air. Join your palms above your head.
- When you breathe out, pop your hands down to your heart center. Your belly should deflate just like a balloon. Practice a few times.
- Now make it fun by wiggling your hands back and forth on the out breath in a strong pop. Repeat ten times.

MILKSHAKE BREATH

Milkshake Breath is so called because the tongue curls into a tube shape like a straw and the inhaled breath feels cold like a milkshake when it enters the body. This is a kid-friendly version of a breathing technique called Sitali breath in adult yoga. Milkshake Breath is best practiced when the weather is warm because it will cool kids off, but it is also a good tool to use anytime children are upset or angry and need to cool off.

Benefits

Milkshake Breath calms hot emotions, such as anger and aggression. Rolling the tongue passes air through the saliva on the tongue, which cools and adds moisture to the body. Milkshake Breath will help settle your child's mind and body so that she feels calm and peaceful.

What to Say

- We are going to practice Milkshake Breath. Milkshake Breath helps us to cool off and calm down. Can you think of a time when you may have needed this breath?
- Roll the tip of your tongue up to touch the roof of your mouth, or stick out your tongue and curl it into a tube shape.
- Breathe in through your mouth as if drinking through a straw, and feel the cool air enter your body. Does it remind you of drinking a milkshake through a straw? Brrrr...it feels cold. Now breathe out slow and long through your nose.
- Repeat ten times. What did you notice? How do you feel?

Mindfulness Challenge

Ask children to notice the difference between how the air feels on the inhale and how it feels on the exhale. Which is warmer?

COUNTING BREATHS

Counting Breaths is a deep breathing exercise that uses counting as an anchor to keep focus on the breath. Counting Breaths is a simple way to practice mindfulness that can be done anywhere. When children are upset, Counting Breaths helps them regain control of their emotions and settle their thoughts. This mindfulness tool can be used when children are feeling anxious, moody, or simply need to relax.

Benefits

Counting Breaths improves focus, creating mindfulness, which leads to feelings of relaxation, clarity, and calm. Counting each exhalation keeps the attention in the present moment.

What to Say

- Did you know that counting your breaths can help you focus? Let's try it.
- Lie on your back with both hands on your belly. Take a deep breath in through your nose.
- Feel your belly rise beneath your hands. As you breathe out, feel your hands fall. Slowly count "ooone" as you release your breath.
- Continue counting and breathing in this way until you get to ten. Still not calm? Try it again. Make sure your breath is reaching all the way to your belly button.
- Sit up very slowly. How do you feel?

Mindfulness Challenge

Have older children find their heartbeat or pulse before and after Counting Breaths. Did their pulse change? Breathing can change how we feel by reducing our heart rate. This challenge introduces children to the concept that they have control over their breathing and heart rate.

ELEVATOR BREATH

This breathing technique is referred to as "three-part breath" because of how the breath enters the abdomen, diaphragm, and chest. Children often breathe with only the top portion of their lungs, which means they are missing out on the benefits of using their entire lungs to breathe. Breathing in and out at full capacity provides a sense of balance and calm.

Benefits

Elevator Breath brings children's awareness to moving their breath to their belly, which helps them to breathe deeper. It activates the brain's relaxation system, which sends an instant calm feeling throughout the body. It is relaxing and reduces stress. Placing their hands on their belly and heart allows children to feel their breath, which helps with focus and mindfulness.

What to Say

- Let's practice Elevator Breath. Sit up tall.
- Place one hand on your heart and one hand on your belly. Notice your breath and your heartbeat. Is it fast, medium, or slow?
- Take a deep breath in through your nose. Feel your belly, rib cage, and heart center rise beneath your hands.
- As you breathe out, feel your belly, rib cage, and heart center fall. Do you feel the elevator going up and down with each breath?
- Start to make your elevator go even slower by making your breath slower. Repeat nine times. Notice your breath and heartbeat. Have they changed?

BRAIN BREATH

Brain Breath is similar to "alternate nostril breathing." Yogic teachings purport that the nostrils are entryways to energy centers in the body. The left nostril is cooling, which is relaxing. The right nostril is warming, which is energizing. Brain Breath is a way to consciously harness both of those benefits.

Benefits

Brain Breath harmonizes the brain hemispheres, which results in emotional well-being. It is calming and improves focus. And it just feels good!

What to Say

- Did you know that breathing through only one nostril can change how you feel? Let's try it. Sit up tall in Easy Seated Pose.
- Roll your shoulders up to your ears and let them fall down your back.
- Gently place your peace fingers (your pointer and middle fingers) on either side of your nose.
- Use your right pointer finger to close your right nostril. Breathe in and out slowly and deeply through your left nostril for three breaths. Notice how you feel.
- Now switch to breathing on your right side while closing off your left nostril. Breathe in slowly for three breaths.
- Notice how you feel.

Mindfulness Challenge

Try Brain Breath again. Ask children to notice which nostril was easier to breathe out of. Then notice which one was warmer. What did they discover?

HOT CHOCOLATE BREATH

Hot Chocolate Breath is a simple breathing technique that uses longer exhales to enhance relaxation. Hot Chocolate Breath extends the exhalation a few seconds longer than the inhale, just like you are blowing on a hot cup of cocoa. When your child's exhale is longer than the inhale, the vagus nerve, a long nerve that travels throughout the body, sends a signal to her brain to relax.

Benefits

Hot Chocolate Breath reduces anxiety, improves mood, and puts the body in a state of calm. It also enhances focus and concentration. When Hot Chocolate Breath is used in yoga, it is referred to as an extended exhale. In yoga, it can move your child gently into a deeper stretch because it helps muscles relax, release, and lengthen.

What to Say

- I love to drink hot chocolate, but sometimes it is too hot, so I have to use my breath to blow on it to cool it off. The longer I can breathe on it, the cooler it becomes. Let's practice Hot Chocolate Breath.
- Begin in Easy Seated Pose with your shoulders rolled back and the top of your head facing the ceiling. Breathe in through your nose, fill up your belly, and count to four (1, 2, 3, 4) in your mind. Pause.
- Now let's cool off the hot chocolate. Slowly breathe out through your mouth as if you are breathing on a cup of hot chocolate, counting in your head to four (1, 2, 3, 4...) and then continuing to five and six (5, 6). Great. It's not quite cool enough to drink. Let's try it again. Repeat at least three times.

Brain Challenge

Add movement and balance to the breath. Place six yoga blocks or stepping stones in a line. The first two blocks should be a different color from the last four blocks. Tell the children, "Stand up tall as you walk across the blocks. Focus so that you don't fall off. Breathe in when you step on the first two blocks and breath out while you step on the last four blocks." Add this variation to Hot Chocolate Breath to an obstacle course for an extra fun twist.

BOX BREATH

Box Breath is a four-part breathing exercise that involves pausing the breath after each inhale and exhale. Box Breath works best if you can show the kids a picture of a square, or box, where each side has an arrow pointing toward a corner. The arrows point upward on the left side, then across the top, then down the right side, and back across the base of the square. Have children follow the arrows with their finger as they breathe. This provides a visual tool to help children remain focused. Use belly breathing, meaning your belly rises on the inhale and falls on the exhale.

Box Breath is best practiced with children who are eight years and older who are familiar with breath work.

Benefits

Box Breath is calming. It helps children self-regulate when they are feeling strong emotions. Providing a visual support helps keep children focused and engaged.

What to Say

- Let's practice a breathing technique called Box Breath. Begin by placing a finger on the bottom left corner of the box.
- Trace the arrow upward with your finger as you breathe in through your nose for a count of four (1, 2, 3, 4...). When you get to the top corner, hold your breath for a count of four (1, 2, 3, 4...) as you trace the arrow across the top of the box.
- Then breathe out as you slide your finger down the box to the count of four (1, 2, 3, 4...). Finally, pause your breath as you trace your finger along the bottom of the box for a count of four (1, 2, 3, 4...).
- Once this ratio feels comfortable, you can make it more challenging by trying to breathe in for a count of five, pause for a count of five, breathe out for a count of five, and then pause again for a count of five. Repeat three or more times. When you are finished, notice how you feel. Is it different than how you felt before you started? How so?

Brain Challenge

Add imagination to this exercise. Tell the children, "For a challenge, try following invisible arrows in the air. Draw a square in the air with your finger. Begin in the lower left corner just as you did on paper."

Mindfulness Variation

It is easy to get creative with Box Breath. For a sensory experience, use shaving cream (or make a batch of instant pudding if kids won't understand not to try to eat the shaving cream). Place shaving cream on a table or cookie sheet. Make a square in the shaving cream with your finger. Maybe even add a few arrows. Kids will love tracing the square in shaving cream while practicing Box Breath. Remember to breathe in for a count of four, pause for a count of four, breathe out for a count of four, pause for a count of four.

For children who like movement, make a giant square out of duct tape, mats, or props on the floor. Make sure each side equals four steps and have children practice Box Breath as they slowly walk around the box.

WHERE IS MY BREATH?

Children love the challenge of trying to figure out where their breath is going in their body. This breathing exercise brings awareness to the breath and the body. Where Is My Breath? teaches children that they can find and control their breath.

Benefits

Deep breathing is calming to the nervous system. In addition, paying attention to the breath keeps children in the present moment so they are not worrying about the future or thinking about the past; they are just focused on their breath.

What to Say

- Did you know you can send your breath anywhere in your body? Try to be very still and mindfully pay attention to where you feel your breath in your body. Ready? Let's try it.
- Lie down on your back in Starfish (Chapter 2). Wiggle your toes and fingers. Wiggle your body a bit to get it ready for being mindful and still.
- Close your eyes. Take a slow, deep breath in. Pause. Let it all out. Place your hand on your belly button. Take a deep breath in. Can you feel it in your belly? What did you feel when it left your belly? Did you notice how your fingers moved apart as you breathed in and came back together as you breathed out? Take another deep breath in. Let it all out.
- Where else did you feel your breath go this time? Was it in your thumb? Your ear? Take another breath in, notice where your breath goes in your body. Slowly come to an Easy Seated Pose. What did you notice?

Mindfulness Challenge

Have children try breathing in different positions, such as lying on their tummies, sitting in Easy Seated Pose, and standing in Mountain Pose. Discuss whether their breath goes to different places in the body if they are in different positions. Ask children to notice which position made it easy or difficult to breathe. (For example, lying on the belly provides resistance, making it more difficult to fill the belly up with air. See if your child notices this.)

BUTTERFLY BREATH

Butterfly Breath is a breathing technique that goes with Butterfly Pose. This calming breathing exercise is great to do first thing in the morning to wake the body up. It's a wonderful way for children of all ages to release stress, stretch, and breathe.

Benefits

Butterfly Breath is a simple way to link breath to movement. Butterfly Breath is a good hip stretch and it provides deep pressure in the form of proprioception, which is calming to the nervous system. It improves posture, coordination, and brain organization, and helps children feel grounded.

What to Say

- Let's breathe like a butterfly. Sit up tall, with your legs in front of you. Bend your knees, let your knees go out, and bring your feet in closer to your body.
- Let's pretend we are spreading glue all over the bottoms of both our feet. Once they are completely covered, pretend to glue them together.
- Now let's make our butterfly beautiful by adding a few stripes and some glitter. Start at the feet. Put your right hand on your right foot and your left hand on your left foot. Squeeze your feet between your thumb and other fingers in a stripe. Fantastic! Pretend that there is a bright-colored stripe where your hands touched your feet. Now let's put stripes all over our butterfly. Slowly start to move up your legs, squeezing stripes in as you go.
- Now let's do our arms. Take opposite hands to opposite wrists and start to squeeze up to your shoulders.
- What about our head? Let's put some stripes on our ears. Use your thumb and index finger to slowly put stripes (squeezes) up your ear. Pat the top of your head with both hands. Now let's make our way back down the body. Repeat the process moving down the body.
- Should we put some glitter on our butterfly? Starting at your feet, tap your fingers all over your skin, all the way up your legs, to your arms, shoulders, and head. What a gorgeous butterfly!

- Are you ready to fly? Bring your hands together at your heart with palms touching. Sit up tall. As you breathe in, raise your hands above your head. Pause. As you breathe out, separate your hands, rolling your wrists outward, and send your arms out wide. Slowly push them all the way to the floor, to flap your wings. Repeat ten times.
- My butterfly is tired from all that flying. Let's take a nap. Keeping your feet glued together, slowly lean forward for Sleeping Butterfly. Take a few deep breaths while you sleep. Roll up very slowly. Release your legs and shake them out in front of you. Notice how you feel.

Breathing Props

Breathing exercises can be tough for younger kids, who can get distracted relatively quickly. These props will keep them interested and focused.

BREATHING WITH BUBBLES

Bubbles are a great introduction to mindfulness for young children. Wedding-favor bubble solution comes in small bottles that are easy for small hands to hold. The mixture also contains more glycerin, and doesn't require as much force to blow bubbles, making it the perfect mindfulness tool for little ones.

Materials

- Bubble solution

Benefits

Bubbles calm and center children. Breathing with Bubbles encourages children to practice deep breathing, which has a calming effect. For young children, the act of blowing bubbles strengthens the muscles in the mouth, improving speech and language skills.

What to Say

- Sit up tall at the back of your yoga mat. Take a deep breath in. Fill your belly up with air.
- Breathe out slowly into the bubble wand. Good breathing!
- Let's have a contest! Try to blow bubbles so that they float all the way to the other end of your mat. Remember, breathe long and slow for this contest. Ready? Let's breathe.

Mindfulness Challenge

Bubbles are a fun way to release stress and any emotion your child needs to let go of. Tell the children, "Start in Easy Seated Pose. Close your eyes. Are you feeing sad, grumpy, or mad? Notice the feeling. Open your eyes. Bring the bubble wand in front of your mouth. Take a deep breath in, fill your tummy with air. Now blow all those icky feelings into your bubbles. Let them float away. Do this ten more times to make sure you blow them all away. Close your eyes. Notice how you feel. Can you put a smile on your face?"

PINWHEELS

Pinwheels are a fun and simple toy made of plastic or aluminum curls attached to a stick. Pinwheels spin when your child blows on them, making them a fantastic tool to demonstrate the power of the breath.

Benefits

Using pinwheels as a visual prop is calming and helps children focus on their breath. Blowing a pinwheel shows your child the strength and length of their breath. Pinwheels can help disperse stress and excess energy.

What to Say

- Hold your pinwheel sideways.
- Take a deep breath in through your nose.
- Make sure the breath reaches your belly, making it become bigger.
- Now make your lips into a circle, like you're about to whistle. Slowly blow on your pinwheel. Keep going!
- Practice a couple of long exhalations, then we'll have a contest. Let's see whose pinwheel can spin the longest. Ready. Set. Go!

Mindfulness Challenge

Tell the children, "Blow your pinwheel while in Tree Pose. Tree Pose improves focus, concentration, and balance. Adding the pinwheel adds an element of mindfulness. Begin in Mountain Pose with your hands together at your heart center holding the pinwheel. Bring the pinwheel out in front of you to use as a focal point. When you are ready, shift your weight to one foot. Turn the opposite foot out, resting your big toe on the ground and resting your heel on your other ankle. Take a deep breath in through the nose. Exhale through your lips. Watch the pinwheel spin. Repeat two more times. Now try it on the other side. Come back to Mountain Pose. What did you notice? Was one side easier than the other?"

Brain Challenge

Tell the children, "Walk around the room, holding your pinwheel with one hand (and blowing it) and tapping your thigh with the other hand. Switch sides. Come back to Mountain Pose. Take a deep breath in. Let it out. What did you notice?"

HOBERMAN SPHERE

The Hoberman Sphere is also called the breathing sphere because it is an isokinetic structure with movable joints that starts small and grows larger, just as your belly does when you do belly breathing. Not only do the spheres come in various sizes, but some even glow in the dark. The Hoberman Sphere is a great way to show your child how the belly fills with air when she breathes in and empties when she breathes out.

Benefits

The Hoberman Sphere is a great teaching tool. It provides children with a visual representation of how to breathe. The Hoberman Sphere encourages focus and breath awareness. The motion of the sphere is almost magically relaxing. It reduces anxiety and is calming.

What to Say

- Sit up tall in Easy Seated Pose. Take a deep breath, and fill your belly with air as you expand the sphere.
- Breathe out as you close the sphere.
- Continue breathing in and out slowly and evenly eight more times.

Mindfulness Variation

To add an extra dose of calm to an obstacle course, lock a giant Hoberman Sphere open and have children carefully climb into the center. Once in the center, have them hold a small sphere and take five deep breaths, moving the sphere in and out, too, before returning to the obstacle course. This centers children and incorporates mindfulness into an active course, which teaches self-regulation.

FEATHER WEATHER

This breathing exercise uses a feather and is wonderful for children of all ages. The weather that is given to the feather comes from the breath. After each stage of weather, encourage your child to share his experience.

Benefits

Feather Weather introduces children to the concept that our breath can change how we feel. Since it uses different breathing techniques, it can be both calming and energizing. Feather Weather encourages awareness of the breath and promotes connectedness.

What to Say

- We are going to give our feathers some different kinds of weather. Lie on your back. Bring your feather in front of your mouth.
- Take a deep breath in through your nose.
- As you breathe out through your mouth, practice blowing your feather. Now let's release our feather and see if we can blow our breath to keep it floating above our heads.
- Now give your feather some weather:
  - Start with a soft summer breeze. Slowly and gently blow your feather into the air.
  - Next, try a tornado. This is a more powerful breath that moves in a circle. Breathe through pursed lips forcefully.
  - Can you blow your feather in a circle? There's a hurricane outside and things are blowing all over. Take a deep breath in through your nose and blow it out in short bursts through your mouth.
- Notice how each different breathing style makes you feel. How does a hurricane make you feel? Which breath makes you feel calm?

PARACHUTE BREATH

As most physical education teachers have discovered, children enjoy playing with parachutes. Using a parachute to teach children how to breathe is not only fun, but gives them a visual to help them learn how to breathe from the diaphragm. Parachute Breath is best done with at least four children ages five and up.

Benefits

Parachute Breath teaches children how different breathing patterns can affect how they feel. This breathing activity helps the body and mind relax while children have fun with different breathing techniques.

What to Say

- Let's sit in a circle around the edges of the parachute.
- Come into Easy Seated Pose. Grab hold of the edges of the parachute.
- Make ripples with the parachute. Good! Now let's slowly make the parachute go up and down by raising our arms all the way up to the height of the top of our head.
- Great! Now let's begin to match our breath to how we move the parachute. Make ripples. As the parachute goes up, we inhale, making our bellies big. As the parachute moves down, we let our breath out, making our bellies flat.
- Now let's slow it down. Continue to breathe with the parachute, inhaling as we lift and exhaling with the fall. What did you notice? Did breathing slow make you feel different than breathing fast?

BEANIE BREATH

For this exercise, Teenie Beanies, which are miniature and less expensive Beanie Babies, work best. These small stuffed animals are perfect for placing on a child's belly. Teenie Beanies are also helpful if your child is feeling scared or nervous going someplace new. They provide comfort, making transitions easier.

Benefits

Beanie Breath teaches children to become aware of their breath. The weight of the beanie adds resistance and encourages focus. Beanie Breath is calming and relaxing.

What to Say

- We are going to give our beanies a ride. Lie on your back. Relax your body and place your Teenie Beanie on your belly.
- Start to breathe in and out through your nose. Feel your belly rising and falling with your breath, giving your beanie a ride. Now see if you can breathe a little slower and deeper.
- Can you feel your beanie moving with your breath? Repeat ten times. Open your eyes, take a deep breath, and smile.

Mindfulness Variation

Say to the children, "Get to know your Teenie Beanie. What does he look like? How does he feel? Soft, hard? What color is he? Does he have a name?"

Breathing Games

Standard seated or standing breathing exercises are always great to try, but some days, your children might need a little more structure and movement to stay interested. Try these fun games at those times!

PING-PONG RACE

Ping-Pong Race involves blowing air through a straw to move different items a short distance. After a couple of practice rounds, arrange the space so children can have a race on the floor!

Materials

- Ping-Pong balls
- Pom-poms
- Cotton balls
- Yoga mats

Benefits

Ping-Pong Race promotes long exhalations, which are calming to the nervous system. Children are moving on their bellies, which provides resistance when breathing, causing them to use their breath more effectively.

What to Say

- Let's have a race. Come to the back of your mat and lie on your stomach. We are going to practice breathing by trying to move objects to the top of our mats using only our breath.
- Let's start with the pom-pom. Lie on your belly and blow through the straw. Next, try the cotton ball and the Ping-Pong ball.
- Which object was easiest to blow? Why? Remember to emphasize long breaths in and out so your objects move farther.
- Want to try a longer race? Race the objects across the living room or yoga studio.

Bubble Mountain

Bubble Mountain is a simple, calming breathing exercise appropriate for slightly older children who won't be tempted to suck in through the straw. Put approximately two tablespoons of dish soap in the bottom of a bowl. Add about two inches of water to the bowl. Have children put their straws in the water, making sure they are under the water. Have them take a deep breath in through the nose and blow a long exhalation through the straw, forming a Bubble Mountain.

Materials

- Plastic bowl
- Straws
- Dish soap

Benefits

Bubble Mountain is fun and it offers multiple health benefits. It teaches children deep breathing, which helps them relax and reduces stress. Figuring out ways to lengthen the straws (as shown in the Brain Challenge) enhances executive functioning skills, such as problem-solving. Blowing into different sizes of straws (as shown in the Mindfulness Challenge) teaches children awareness of breath and mindfulness.

What to Say

- We are going to make a Bubble Mountain. Put your straw in the water.
- Remember to only blow *out* through the straw. Don't suck in.
- Take a deep breath in through your nose and then let it out slowly through your mouth. Keep making your mountain grow taller. Great breathing!

Brain Challenge

Place extra straws in front of your child. When the bubbles reach the end of the child's straw, ask questions like "How can we make this mountain taller without it popping on our noses?" Try to let your child problem-solve ways that he can keep building his mountain (such as connecting two straws). After a minute or two, ask questions like "Did you notice a difference in the Bubble Mountain when you used two straws instead of one?"

Mindfulness Challenge

First, provide your child with a skinny straw. Have her make a Bubble Mountain. After she has built a mountain, have her stir the mountain up. Now provide her with a wider straw and have her make another Bubble Mountain. Next, have her use both straws together to make the mountain. Ask your child, "Which straw made it easier to build the mountain? Why? Which straw do you prefer?"

Mindfulness Variation

This variation was created by Lindsey Lieneck of Yogapeutics. To encourage an inward focus, have your child wear noise-reducing headphones while she is building the Bubble Mountain. Ask your child questions, such as "How does building a mountain while wearing headphones compare to not using headphones? Is it easier to focus with or without the headphones?"

BUBBLE POP

This a group game appropriate for all ages. Give each child a small bottle of bubble solution. Place the children's mats in a circle. Have one child stand in the center of the mats. This child will pop the bubbles as fast as he or she can. Set a timer for thirty seconds. Have children on the mats blow bubbles to the person standing in the center. Be sure to emphasize that long exhalations make more bubbles. Repeat until all children have had a turn being in the center popping bubbles.

Benefits

Bubble Pop improves mood and is a fun way to practice extending the exhale. Bubble Pop also improves eye-hand coordination skills.

What to Say

- Let's get in a circle. We are going to play a game with bubbles. Who would like to be in the middle of the circle first?
- I'm going to give each of you a bottle of bubble solution. When I say "Go!" you are going to blow bubbles at the child standing in the middle of the circle. The child in the middle of the circle is going to pop the bubbles as fast as he can while counting out loud how many he pops.
- Let's get started. Sit up tall, and take a big breath in through your nose. Breathe out through your mouth very slow and long. Ready? Go!

MINDFUL BREATHING TRAIN

This fun group activity may need a conductor to help organize the herringbone pattern that the children make with their bodies. This breathing exercise helps children to let go of worries and be in the moment. Be wary of doing the breathing train with tween boys and girls as they may feel uncomfortable.

Benefits

The Breathing Train brings attention to the breath. It is a calming exercise that builds community too. Breathing with friends makes children feel good about themselves and makes friendships stronger.

What to Say

- We are going to make a Breathing Train with our bodies. Let's have the first person lie down on her back. The next person lies down and puts his head on the stomach of the first person, and then the next person lies down and puts her head on the stomach of the second person, and so on.
- When the train is assembled, close your eyes and feel your head gently lifting and falling as the person you are resting on breathes in and out. Try to match your breath to the breath of the person that your head is lying on.
- Notice what you hear, feel, and smell. After ten deep, slow breaths, open your eyes and one by one disassemble the train, then slowly rise to Easy Seated Pose. What did you notice during the train?

ANIMAL SAYS

Animals Says is a variation of the game "Simon Says." One child is the leader and demonstrates an animal yoga pose or a movement with animal sounds. Children follow along when the leader says, "Animal says." If the leader does not say, "Animal says" and the player moves, the player remains in Easy Seated Pose until all but one player is left.

Benefits

Children will have fun practicing different breathing techniques, such as panting like a dog, hissing like a snake, and roaring like a lion. The animal poses will enhance strength and flexibility, while listening for "Animal says" will improve concentration and mindfulness.

What to Say

- We are going to play a game called Animal Says. I'll start by being the leader and then we will take turns being the leader.
- I'm going to demonstrate an animal yoga pose or movement with animal sounds. Do the movements and make the sounds, but only when I say, "Animal says." If I do not say, "Animal says" then stay in your current animal position.
- If you accidently do the pose when I didn't say "Animal says" then you'll go into Easy Seated Pose until there is only one player left. Be very mindful and listen for the key words. Ready? Let's begin.

CHAPTER 4

Mindfulness and the Senses

Children learn and develop through their senses. Sensory information comes into our bodies from the world around us. Your child's brain and nervous system process and incorporate the information. Then he uses the sensory messages for purposeful movement, thoughts, and feelings. That's how incorporating senses into mindfulness activities can impact a child's development, both physically and mentally.

Our senses begin to form before we are born and then develop rapidly in early childhood. Most of us are familiar with the basic five senses: vision, hearing, smell, taste, and touch. But did you know there are other senses—proprioception (muscle and joints) and vestibular (movement)? They tell your child how he is stretching, balancing, and moving. These senses help your child achieve developmental milestones, such as crawling and walking. As children grow, their senses integrate more fully and they can learn higher-level skills, such as motor planning, attention span, and emotional stability. This chapter showcases mindful activities that can enhance each sensory system to help your child connect mind and body, improving self-regulation.

Mindful Hearing: The Auditory Sense

Receptors in the inner ear are activated by airwaves. The receptors transmit sound information to the brain for clarification. The auditory sense allows us to hear and discriminate among sounds. This sense is important for learning language and communication skills. Loud, fast sounds are stimulating to children while slow, rhythmic sounds are calming. This means the music you play and noises in the environment can affect your child's mood.

FINDING SOUNDS

When children are busy, they don't notice all the sounds in their environment. Mindfully listening develops awareness by having children sit quietly with their eyes closed for sixty seconds, listening to the sounds around them.

Benefits

Mindful listening is an auditory focusing activity that enhances listening skills, awareness, and focus. Sitting quietly and noticing sounds directs the brain to listen and hear things we normally take for granted, such as the whirr of the ceiling fan or the buzz of the fridge. The more your child practices mindful listening, the better she will become at quieting her mind and calming herself.

What to Say

- Who can tell me what your five senses are? Yes, they are hearing, seeing, feeling, tasting, and smelling. Right now we are going to focus on listening.
- Let's sit up tall in Easy Seated Pose. Take one big Balloon Breath in through the nose. Breathe out; let all the air go.
- Ready to focus? Close your eyes and listen very carefully for all the sounds you can hear. Open your eyes. What did you hear? Did you notice more sounds than you usually do? How did it make you feel?

Mindfulness Challenge

Mindfully listen with your child for thirty seconds while staying indoors. Write down everything you hear. Next, go outdoors and listen for thirty seconds. Again, write down all the sounds. Discuss what you heard. Was it easier to hear sounds inside or outside?

AMBIENT MUSIC

Did you know that music can affect your child's brain and emotions? Amazing, right? Science tells us music enters the ear and activates certain areas of the brain. However, not all children's brains respond the same way. This means that the ways music affects your child can vary. Additionally, research tells us that some types of music are better than others for engaging the brain. Ambient music (music with gentle, soothing tones and no words) is best for creativity, focus, and mood. This simple listening activity uses ambient music to activate the brain for learning. Try having your older child listen to calming ambient music while engaging in mindful breathing for three minutes before completing homework or a task that requires extra attention.

Benefits

Research tells us children learn more effectively when they feel comfortable. This listening activity reduces stress, calms the nervous system, and helps the body and mind to focus. Ambient music primes the brain for learning and creativity.

What to Say

- Find a comfortable position, such as Easy Seated Pose or lying on your back.
- Let's close our eyes. Begin to breathe in and out through your nose. Feel your belly rise when breathing in and fall when breathing out.
- Listen to the music and focus on your breath. How do you feel? Ready to learn?

CHIME LISTENING

This listening activity is a way to engage a child before starting a meditation or any other activity that requires a child to be calm and relaxed. Chime Listening involves listening for as long you can to a chime or a similar sound that slowly fades. As the sound fades, your child indicates silently, by raising his hand, when he can no longer hear the sound. It's important to let your child know that what he just did was mindfulness—paying attention, with his senses, so he can choose his behavior.

Materials

- Chime (can be purchased inexpensively online)

Benefits

Chime Listening is a great way to introduce the concept of mindfulness. When Chime Listening is practiced frequently, with the same sound, it engages the brain to connect more easily with the sound. This results in increased attention and being mindful in the moment.

What to Say

- Sit up tall in Easy Seated Pose or lie down on your back. We are going to listen with our senses. When you hear the chime, listen as long and carefully as you can. When we can't hear the chime any longer we are going to raise our hands, keeping our eyes closed. Ready?
- Close your eyes. Listen. After your child has raised his hand say, "Great focusing!" Did you know the listening practice you just did was mindfulness? When you focused your attention on the chime, you were being mindful.

Mindfulness Variation

In a classroom setting, do this activity twice. The first time the teacher will ring the chime. The second time a child who was actively listening will ring the chime. Children love ringing the chime! Giving a child the opportunity to ring the chime will increase focus and participation.

Mindfulness Challenges

For older children, ask them to count their breath using Counting Breaths, from Chapter 3: Mindful Breathing. Instead of simply raising their hands, have them show how many breaths they took by holding up the same number of fingers. Remind them to take slow, deep breaths. The goal is not to have the most breaths.

HAPPY LISTENING

Happy Listening is a partner activity for elementary school-aged children. This activity is a variation of an aerial yoga activity created by Lindsey Lieneck of Yogapeutics. It involves listening to the song "Happy" by Pharrell Williams. Every time you hear the word "happy," touch palms with your partner and spin in a circle.

Benefits

This activity has multiple sensory benefits that help stimulate the brain. Spinning engages your child's vestibular system while the handclap engages the proprioceptive and tactile systems. Happy listening also helps with impulse control and increases mindful awareness.

What to Say

- Face your partner. Hold up your hands so your palms are facing your partner's palms, but don't touch palms yet.
- I am going to play a song. Every time you hear the word "happy," clap hands with your partner and turn around in a circle once.
- The next time you hear the word "happy," clap and turn again, but go the opposite direction. Remember, only clap and turn when you hear the word "happy."

Mindful Smelling: The Olfactory Sense

Receptors in our nose allow us to smell and determine the differences between various smells. Our sense of smell is linked to our limbic system, which is a system of nerves in the brain concerned with strong emotions and memory. What is unique about our olfactory sense is that when we smell something, it follows a direct path to the limbic system, whereas our other senses take the scenic route. This means our response to smell is immediate, and it is why smell, more than any other sense, can trigger emotional memories in children. Smells such as lavender and vanilla are calming while smells such as peppermint are energizing. However, different scents have different effects on different children, so it's always best to use caution when doing Mindful Smelling in a group.

SMELL AND TELL

Smell and Tell is appropriate for children ages five and up. For this game, find five small containers that are a little bigger than a cotton ball and not too deep. Put a couple of drops of essential oil on each of the cotton balls and drop them in the cups. (Each cotton ball should have a different oil.) Therapeutic-grade essential oils (e.g., lemon, lime, orange, and balsam fir) work well for this activity. If you don't have essential oils, raid the pantry and use vanilla, vinegar, pickle juice, lemon juice, or cinnamon sticks. Try to use scents that children are familiar with and stick to scents that are either calming *or* energizing—don't mix calming and energizing scents together. Everyone takes turns smelling the cotton ball in the container. Once everyone has had a turn smelling, the guessing begins. Ask children to write their guesses on a piece of paper and then discuss the guesses at the end of the activity.

Materials

- Five small glass containers, like airplane-approved travel-size containers
- Cotton balls
- Essential oils
- Paper and writing utensil

Benefits

Smell and Tell, especially when used with essential oils, may improve memory and help children relax. Using their sense of smell makes children more aware of their environment, which enhances focus and attention. Talking about what the scents remind them of promotes communication skills. Writing or drawing their responses improves fine motor skills.

What to Say

- Start by sitting in Easy Seated Pose. We are going to try to identify some different scents. Reach inside the glass in front of you and bring the cotton ball up to your nose and sniff. Put it back in the glass when you're done smelling.
- Write or draw on your paper what you think the scent is. Don't say what it is yet.
- Carefully pass the glass to the child sitting next to you.
- OK, now that everyone is done, what do you think the scent was? What did it remind you of? How did it make you feel?
- Repeat this process with the other scents.

Mindfulness Challenge

Take the cotton balls out of the container. Have your child smell both the container and the cotton balls and try to figure out which cotton ball goes in which container.

NOSE PLUG

You might know that our sense of smell is linked to our sense of taste, but kids might not. The nose plug test is a great way to teach children how their senses are related. This activity requires organic jelly beans. (Food dyes in regular jelly beans are harmful to children, as is processed sugar, but organic jelly beans are made with real fruit juices and colors from natural sources. They are also gluten-, fat-, and peanut-free.) Find two jelly beans of the same flavor. Ask your child to eat the first jelly bean with her nose plugged. Next have her eat the same flavor without her nose plugged. Mindfully discuss the differences.

Materials

- Organic jelly beans

Benefits

Approximately 75 percent of taste is based on our sense of smell. This activity teaches children their sense of taste and smell are linked. Chewing jelly beans provides sensory input to the jaw by using jaw muscles. Children's mindful awareness is increased by focusing on the senses while eating the two jelly beans.

What to Say

- We are going to do a taste test with jelly beans! But first let's use our senses to explore this jelly bean. What do you see? What do you feel?
- Plug your nose. Eat the jelly bean. What do you taste?
- Let's mindfully explore our second jelly bean. Does it look similar to our first jelly bean? Yes, it looks and feels the same. Bring it up to your nose. What does it smell like? Let's taste it. What do you notice? How did plugging your nose change how it tasted?

SCRATCH-AND-SNIFF STICKERS

You can make your own scratch-and-sniff stickers at home. Using a label maker or printable label sheets, you can create and print out lemons, peppermints, limes, and flower labels. Next, apply one drop of 100 percent therapeutic-grade oil with a cotton swab to each corresponding picture. (Put the oil on the swabs ahead of time—don't let children handle the oil containers.) The ink may bleed a little. Once the stickers are dry, your child will love putting them on envelopes, cards, or even a bookmark.

Materials

- Circular labels
- Printable file for labels
- Essential oils
- Printer
- Ink

Benefits

Different essential oils have different benefits. Lavender, lime, orange, and lemon essential oils have been known to balance the body and have a calming effect. Essential oils improve focus and promote a sense of well-being. Additionally, aromas can bring peace and happiness to the mind and body.

What to Say

- We are going to make our own scratch-and-sniff stickers. What are four of your favorite smells? Lemon, lime, peppermint, and orange are great choices!
- I've printed out stickers that go with your choices. Now for the fun part—let's make them smell amazing.
- Take the orange cotton swab and rub it over the orange stickers. Great!
- Let's put lemon on our lemon stickers. Fantastic. Now it's time for lime. Here is a lime-scented cotton swab. Remember to rub it all over the sticker.
- Rub peppermint all over the peppermint stickers. Yum! This one reminds me of mint chocolate chip ice cream. What does it remind you of?

Mindful Seeing: The Visual Sense

Your child's visual system is very complex. Retina receptors are activated by light and transmit information to the brain about what we see. Our visual system has muscles and focusing mechanisms, which help your child write and detect differences between faces. Visual input can change how your child feels. Your child may feel calmer in uncluttered rooms with pastel colors and natural lighting. Cluttered rooms that are highly decorated with bold colors can be overstimulating. These activities will encourage your child to look around thoughtfully and carefully.

PING-PONG SEARCH

For this mindfulness activity, you will need a ball pit and lots of balls. This is fun for all ages and can be completed alone or with a partner. Hide ten Ping-Pong balls in a ball pit that's filled with crushproof balls. Have your child get into the ball pit. (If you don't have a ball pit, they are easy to make out of inflatable pools or even large plastic storage containers.) Encourage your child to use her visual and tactile senses to look for the hidden balls. If she has a partner, set a timer and discuss how working together makes it easier to attain goals.

Materials

- Ball pit, large plastic storage container, or small inflatable swimming pool
- Crushproof balls
- Ping-Pong balls

Benefits

This activity builds teamwork when practiced with a partner. It improves mindful awareness, focus, and visual discrimination.

What to Say

- There are ten Ping-Pong balls hidden in this ball pit. We are going to use mindfulness to find them.
- What is mindfulness? Which sense will we be using the most? Correct, our mindful seeing sense. Will we use any other senses? Yes, that's right, our sense of touch. Are you ready? Let's start looking!

SEE AND SPIN

See and Spin is a multisensory activity for all ages. The object is for children to notice all the blue objects in a room. Have your children stand in the middle of a room and slowly turn in a circle in both directions. Whenever children are spinning, make sure they always spend time going in both directions to keep the body and brain balanced. While they are turning, ask them to notice all the blue objects in the room. Once they are through spinning, they will close their eyes and tell you as many blue objects as they can.

Benefits

See and Spin promotes visual working memory, which is an important cognitive skill. It also engages the vestibular system (which provides a sense of balance and spatial orientation), which can strengthen the nervous system. Mindful awareness is enhanced by looking for all the blue objects in the room.

What to Say

- Colors are all around us. Today we are going to focus on blue.
- When I say "Go," we are going to turn *slowly* in one direction, noticing all the blue objects in the room. Then we are going to turn the opposite direction, again noticing all the blue objects. Look mindfully around you. Once you are done spinning, close your eyes. Take a deep breath through your nose. Let all the breath out.
- How many blue things did you see?

FRUIT BOWL

Fruit Bowl is bowling with a twist. Instead of using bowling balls, this game incorporates fruit and mindfulness. Fruit Bowl can be played almost anywhere, at school, yoga class, or even on the kitchen floor.

Materials

- Citrus fruit (such as lemons, limes, clementines, and grapefruits)
- Bowling pins (inflatable pins work best)

Benefits

Fruit Bowl improves balance, perception, and gross and fine motor skills. Aiming and rolling the fruit improves eye-movement skills, such as focusing and tracking. It also provides exercise, which improves heart rate and blood/oxygen circulation.

What to Say

- Sit up tall in Easy Seated Pose. Close your eyes and hold out your palm. I'm going to put a piece of fruit in your hand. Go ahead and touch it. What does it feel like? Is it heavy, light? Is it rough, smooth? What is the shape? Bring it up to your noses. Does it have a smell? Is it sweet, sour? Bring it up to your ear. Does it make a sound?
- Can you guess what it is? Open your eyes. What do you see? Close your eyes again; we have a couple more to examine.
- Now that we have mindfully explored our fruit bowling balls, we are going to gently roll them and try to knock down the bowling pins. We're going to eat them next, so take good care of them! Each time we will use a different fruit to see which one makes the best citrus bowling ball. Let's begin.
- Which citrus bowling ball was your favorite? Why?
- Now let's mindfully eat the fruit. Yum!

FIND THE YOGA JOES

Find the Yoga Joes is a low-key, fun activity for families to play. This activity requires Yoga Joes, which are little army men toys doing yoga poses that can be purchased online. If purchasing Joes isn't in your budget, make your own. Take pipe cleaners and make them into yoga poses. Next, hide your yoga figurines around the house. Have your child look for the yoga figure, and when he finds one, he strikes that pose. Have him put each figure back in their yoga studio as he finds them. (Yoga Joes come with a studio. If your child makes his own yoga figurines, he can make a studio as well. Just decorate a rectangular piece of cardboard, card stock, or notebook paper.)

Materials

- Yoga Joes or pipe cleaners
- Rectangular piece of card stock or cardboard

Benefits

Looking for yoga figures improves focusing and visual discrimination. Bending and reaching for the figures provides vestibular input (movement). Engaging in yoga poses builds strength and flexibility. It also provides exercise, which improves heart rate and blood/oxygen circulation.

What to Say

- Yoga Joes like to hide when they do yoga. Your job is to find each Yoga Joe and do the pose with him. Then place him back in his studio with his friends.
- We are going to take three deep breaths in through our nose and out through our nose with each pose. Ready? Go.

Mindful Tasting: The Gustatory Sense

Tasting something involves many parts of the body. Chemical receptors on the tongue differentiate between flavors and textures. Oral motor input (in the form of blowing or sucking) can further stimulate the brain and nervous system. This means that chewing, sucking, and blowing can change how a child feels. For example, if your child is feeling tired, sucking on a peppermint may wake him up. If he is stressed, drinking a smoothie through a straw may be calming. Typically, foods that are crunchy, sour, cold, or salty are stimulating while foods that are warm and chewy are calming. For more on mindful tasting, read the next chapter, Eating Mindfully.

LEMON WATER

Water is essential for life, but it seems remarkably plain and...unremarkable, if you're not looking at it mindfully. When your children begin to examine it mindfully, they will discover that it is colorless, odorless, and tasteless. Yet it is still so important to our bodies. This fun exercise allows your children to be mindful detectives. First, they'll mindfully take a drink of just plain old water. Then they will mindfully explore a second glass of water that has something added to it. The trick is to have your child use his senses to detect what is different about the second drink of water. Make sure to take the lemon out before your child sees it.

Materials

- Glass of water
- Glass of water with a slice of lemon
- Straws

Benefits

This exercise teaches children about the importance of water, which maintains the balance of body fluids and makes all of the body's systems work better. This exercise enhances mindful awareness by bringing attention to something that most of us don't typically notice, but we use every day.

What to Say

- We are going to be mindful detectives. Hold your cup in your hand. Notice how it feels. Is the cup heavy or light?
- Look at the surface of the liquid. Is it smooth or rippled? Notice how it smells. Take a small drink. Focus on how it tastes and feels in your mouth.
- Pick up the second cup. Look at the surface. Is it different from the surface of the first cup? How so? How does it smell? Take a small drink. Again, focus on how it tastes. Do you notice a difference between this water and the water in the first cup? What is different? Can you guess what has changed?

Mindful Feeling: The Tactile Sense

The tactile sense provides information through our skin. This sense tells us if something is touching us or if we are touching something. We have the most tactile receptors in our mouths and hands, which is why babies are always putting things in their mouths. These exercises will help your child use his tactile sense in new ways.

SPAGHETTI POSE

All you need for Spaghetti Pose is cooked spaghetti and pictures of poses for anyone unfamiliar with yoga. Put a picture of a yoga pose in the middle of the table. Have your child re-create the pose out of two spaghetti noodles. Once the Spaghetti Pose is complete, do the pose. Take three deep breaths on each side before moving on to the next Spaghetti Pose. Try to add poses from different yoga categories, such as balancing, heart opening, standing, and seated postures.

Materials

- Cooked spaghetti
- Yoga pose cards or pictures of yoga poses

Benefits

Spaghetti Pose enhances creativity and fine motor skills while improving tactile discrimination. It is a fun way to practice yoga poses and deep breathing and provides exercise, which increases the heart rate.

What to Say

- Let's make yoga poses out of spaghetti. But first let's explore our spaghetti using our mindfulness skills.
- Put your hands in the bowl of spaghetti. What do you feel? Is it hard, soft? Bring it up to your nose. What do you smell? Should we taste a piece?
- Look at the yoga pose card. What yoga pose do you see? Let's make these two strands of spaghetti into Tree Pose (Chapter 2). That's a fantastic tree!
- Now let's practice being trees ourselves. Make your body look just like the Spaghetti Pose. Take three deep breaths. Repeat on the other side.

MINDFULNESS/MINDLESSNESS

Fill three plastic containers with rice, beans, and pasta. Hide ten mindful and mindless statements in each of the containers. For example, you could write "Trying a new food" or "Picking up after yourself" for mindful statements, and "Trying to do too many things at the same time" or "Texting while walking across the street" for mindless statements. Have your child find the mindful and mindless statements one at a time. Read them together and decide whether they are mindful or mindless.

Materials

- Small plastic containers
- Dry foods (rice, beans, pasta)
- Strips of mindful/mindless statements

Benefits

Playing with dry food promotes tactile discrimination and just feels good! Finding the statements and categorizing them is a fun way to teach children about mindfulness.

What to Say

- Let's place our hands in one of the containers. Feels good!
- Pull out one of the strips of paper. What does it say? Is that a mindful act or a mindless act? Correct, let's place it in the mindfulness pile.
- Let's try another container. What did you find? Hmmm...is that mindful behavior? Let's see if we can find all ten statements!

Mindful Movement: The Vestibular Sense

The vestibular sense is in the inner ear and it detects balance, changes in head position, and movement. The vestibular system has a powerful effect on the body. Vestibular information can stay in the nervous system for hours—that's why you feel like you're still rocking on a boat even when you get back on land. Because of this powerful effect, have children perform the activities in this section only a few times before moving on. Also, if the activity involves spinning, be sure your child is in a safe space to do so, and spins in both directions to balance the brain and the body. Have him spin a few times slowly, as too much spinning can be bad for the brain.

AIRPLANE RIDE

Airplane Ride is an activity that encourages physical contact between you and your child. It is a fun, interactive way to move with your child. Your small child will be the airplane and you will be the wind, giving him a ride.

Benefits

Airplane Ride builds trust and emotional security. Changing head position and moving in different directions provides input to the vestibular system. This activity also builds motor planning skills and body awareness. Keep in mind that Airplane Ride can be stimulating rather than calming.

What to Say

- Would you like an Airplane Ride? Take hold of my hands. I'm going to lie on my back and put my feet on your belly.
- Are you ready to fly? I'm going to be the wind. On three we will take off...three, two, one, liftoff!
- Can you straighten your airplane's tail (the child's legs)? Great. Let's soar higher!

WHEELBARROW RIDE

Wheelbarrow Ride can be done with a friend or parent. Wheelbarrow Ride may not be appropriate for children under five, as they don't have the core and arm strength necessary to hold themselves up. A good prerequisite is to be able to hold a stable plank pose with strong arms. Make sure the wheelbarrow turns her hands inward to reduce overextending at the elbow joint.

Benefits

Wheelbarrow Ride strengthens and provides stability for the core and upper body. Children must focus and shift their weight as they are moving forward or they will crash their wheelbarrow into the floor; therefore this activity promotes body awareness and mindfulness too. Wheelbarrow Ride provides sensory input to the proprioception and vestibular systems for both partners. Due to all the steps and planning involved, this is a great exercise to enhance executive functioning skills.

What to Say

- Begin in Plank Pose. Make sure your fingers are spread wide like starfish, and your wrists are right under your shoulders. Turn your fingers in toward each other.
- I'm going to lift your ankles up as you come up onto your hands. (For children with less core and upper-body strength, hold their body above the knees or at their hips until they gain more core strength.)
- Lean toward the left, putting your weight on your left hand. As you do so, pick up your right hand and move it forward. Repeat on the other side. Great! You are walking on your hands! Where should we walk your wheelbarrow?

Mindfulness Challenge

Make the wheelbarrow race more challenging with a Teenie Beanie. Tell the children, "Find a partner and decide who is going to be the wheelbarrow first. Make sure your partner is about your size. You don't want the wheelbarrow to be too heavy to push. Place the Teenie Beanie on the wheelbarrow's back. When you hear me say 'Go,' mindfully race to the end of the room. Remember the object of the game is to get your Teenie Beanie to the other side of the room. If your Beanie falls off your back, you will have to start over."

HAMMOCK SWING

Hammock Swing can be done with a blanket or using an actual yoga hammock. If using a blanket, your child will be on his back in the center of a strong blanket. One adult will hold the blanket at the feet and one will hold it above your child's head. The adults will lift the blanket at the same time and then gently swing it back and forth. (The child should not engage in active movement while in the hammock.) If you own a hammock or aerial yoga hammock, your child can climb in it safely and lie on his back.

Materials

- Aerial yoga hammock or sturdy blanket
- Two adults

Benefits

Hammock Swing provides deep pressure to any parts of the body that come into contact with the swing, which tends to be calming. The gentle swinging motion provides input to the vestibular system, which is relaxing.

What to Say

- We are going to make a hammock out of this blanket. Lie on your back in the center of the blanket. We are going to lift you up on the count of three and gently rock you back and forth. One, two, three.
- Place your hands on your tummy and take a deep breath in. Feel your tummy rise. Let your breath release slowly through your nose. Feel your tummy fall. Keep breathing in this way as you sway back and forth.

Mindful Deep Pressure: The Proprioceptive Sense

Proprioceptive receptors are present in the muscles, tendons, and joints. The proprioception sense tells children how they are stretching, what they are doing, and where they are in space. This helps them coordinate movements on both sides of the body. This sense is activated with deep pressure. It is also called "heavy work." That's why the following activities include pushing, pulling, massages, and carrying weighted objects.

THE WALL IS FALLING

This deep pressure activity is appropriate for children of all ages. It can be done anywhere there is a wall. It is a great distraction if children are struggling with transitions or just need a little movement. We'll add some mindfulness to it by bringing attention to the senses.

Benefits

Using parts of the body to "hold up the wall" promotes body awareness. Deep pressure provides input to the proprioceptive system. When completed in a group setting, it builds teamwork too.

What to Say

- Oh, no! I think that wall is falling. Hurry! We need to hold it up. Press your hands against the wall.
- Spread your fingers wide so you can hold up more of the wall. Use your strength and push!
- We've been pushing for ten seconds, but it's still falling. I have an idea. Let's turn around and push the back of our entire body against it. What do you feel? Is it cold, warm? Soft, hard? What do you smell? Okay, I think it's solid now. We can let go and relax.

CRASH PAD

A storebought crash pad is a large, thick pad filled with foam. If you don't have a crash pad, make your own out of four to five cushions or a giant beanbag. Children enjoy jumping, crashing, and doing yoga poses on it. The crash pad can also be used for relaxation—for example, to lie on and just breathe. Crashing can be both calming and stimulating, so pay close attention to your child's behavior afterward.

Materials

- Crash pad or four to five large cushions

Benefits

Landing on the crash pad provides deep pressure to the muscles and joints, which activates the proprioceptive system. Crash pads improve mindful attention and core strength, and provide deep pressure. Most important, the kids find creative ways to land, which builds motor planning skills. The mindfulness challenge improves rhythm and timing, which helps with impulse control.

What to Say

- We are going to practice jumping onto the crash pad. Jump onto the pad. Roll off. Begin again.
- Try different ways of jumping, such as a spinning jump or landing on your knees. Do whatever feels good, as long as it's safe!

Mindfulness Challenge

Set a metronome at forty to sixty beats a minute. If you don't own a metronome, play the song "The Ants Go Marching"; it has sixty beats a minute. Clap with the beat. Have your child stand or dance on the crash pad and jump every time he hears a clap. Remember, he should only jump when he hears the clap. This exercise can also be done on a trampoline.

THUNDERSTORM

This activity is taught as part of the Radiant Child Yoga program. It is a fun way for children of all ages to reduce excess energy. Your child will use his body to make a thunderstorm that grows in intensity and then slowly blows over, leaving big puddles on the ground. After the storm, the puddles will be cleaned up by the street cleaner, which is an exercise ball that will roll over your child to provide an extra dose of calm.

Benefits

Patting the thighs and running provide deep impact to the joints and muscles, which is calming and organizing to the nervous system. Thunderstorm teaches children to compare the signals their body sends after exercise and deep breathing. This, in turn, begins to teach them self-regulation skills. When children develop an understanding of the brain–body relationship, they become aware of the messages that their body is sending and are better able to manage their emotions.

What to Say

- Let's stand up. We are going to make a Thunderstorm with our bodies. Before we begin, place a hand on your heart. Close your eyes. Notice your heartbeat and your breath. Are they slow or fast?
- Start to walk in a circle around the outside of the room. Let's make some rain. Gently slap the tops of your legs, making a raindrop sound.
- It's starting to rain harder. Walk a little faster and pat the tops of your legs a little harder.
- Now it's a downpour. Run really fast and and forcefully pat your legs.
- What does thunder sound like? Let's make thunder and lightning sounds. Keep going.
- The rain is starting to slow down. Walk on your tiptoes, making gentle raindrop pats on your legs.
- There are only a few raindrops falling now. Take giant steps, bending your front knee, like a lunge, to make it over the puddles of water. Very slowly pat your legs.

- The rain has finally stopped, leaving big puddles everywhere. Just like a raindrop, slowly float to the floor and make your body into a big puddle by spreading your arms and legs out. Breathe in and out through your nose. Lie very still and keep breathing.
- Now the street cleaner is going to roll over you. Whew, that's done. Now slowly sit up. Notice your heartbeat and your breath. Are they slow or fast? Did they change from the beginning of the storm? Were your body and mind working together?

CHAPTER 5

Eating Mindfully

Hippocrates is considered the father of medicine. He famously stated, "Let food be thy medicine and medicine be thy food." He believed that eating whole foods is the basis for good health. Most caregivers find that what your child eats can make a difference in how he or she feels. Healthy foods like fruits and vegetables provide children with minerals and vitamins, which fuel their brains and all their bodily functions and systems. Encourage kids to think about the saying "You are what you eat" and to eat foods that come from nature and boost overall health.

Mindful Eating

Mindful eating is paying attention to what you are eating, noticing how you feel, and eating with intention. When children learn to eat mindfully, they slow down, savor every bite, and are aware of how much they are eating. Did you know it takes the brain ten minutes to feel full? Slowing down to allow yourself to better gauge your hunger level can have a huge impact on eating habits.

MINDFUL TASTE TEST

Toddlers find food wondrous—they smash it, throw it, and smear it everywhere. However, adults devour it while driving, working, watching TV, or looking at their phone. This mindless eating takes the joy out of eating. Mindful eating is about eating intentionally, slowly, and paying attention to what you are eating with all your senses.

Materials

- Snap peas or other healthy food to taste

Benefits

Mindful eating is simply paying attention, with senses, to the process of eating. Mindful eating is a way for children to practice bringing their attention into the present moment. It improves focus, enhances sense awareness, and promotes digestion.

What to Say

- Mindful eating is a way to use your senses to pay attention while eating. Take a moment to notice the food in your hands with your senses. Is it heavy or light? Warm or cool? Smooth or bumpy? What do you notice about the shape? What does it smell like?
- What is happening in your mind as you smell this object? Does it remind you of something?
- Now close your eyes and bring your attention to just yourself and your food. Is it juicy? Sweet or sour?
- Take one bite at a time, paying attention to what is happening in your mouth.

APPLE TASTE TEST

Compare green apples to red appies. While they may both be apples, they are very different in taste, color, and even health benefits. Give each child a green apple slice and a red apple slice. Have children mindfully sample both. Do they smell different? Which was sweeter?

Materials

- Granny Smith apple
- Red apple, any variety

Benefits

A mindful taste test can help children identify discrete flavors and learn healthy eating habits. It teaches children that when tasted mindfully, apples have very distinct characteristics, making them very different from one another. This activity also encourages children to think carefully about what they are tasting, which trains the brain to pay attention, absorb facts, and think clearly.

What to Say

- We are going to have an apple taste test! Sit up tall. Take a deep Balloon Breath. Let it out.
- Apples are good for us. Have you heard the saying, "An apple a day keeps the doctor away"? What does that mean? Correct, eating apples can make us healthier so we don't have to go to the doctor as much!
- Take a moment to notice the red apple slice in your hands with your senses. Is it heavy or light? Warm or cool? Smooth or bumpy? What do you notice about the shape? What does it smell like? What do you see?
- Take one bite at time, paying attention to what is happening in your mouth. What did it taste like?
- Let's mindfully taste the green apple now. What does it smell like? What do you see?
- Take one bite at a time, paying attention to what is happening in your mouth. What did it taste like?
- How was the green slice different from the red?

TRIPLE TASTE TEST

Triple Taste Test is comparing three pieces of fruit that have been processed in different ways. One piece of fruit is dried, one piece is freeze-dried, and the last piece is raw. Children mindfully compare them using their senses and then discuss the similarities, differences, and health benefits of each.

Materials

- Fruit in dried, freeze-dried, and raw forms

Benefits

Children become aware of the differences in taste and texture. This activity also increases their awareness of how the health benefits of fruit might differ depending on the fruit's form.

What to Say

- We are going to have a Triple Taste Test. We have three pieces of pineapple: one that has been freeze-dried, one that has been dried, and one that is fresh.
- Let's start with the fresh piece of pineapple. What do you see? How does it feel? What do you smell? Let's taste it. What is the texture? How does it taste?
- Now let's try the dried piece of fruit. Dried fruit is just fruit that has been dried out. However, when you buy dried fruit, be sure to check the package to make sure it is just fruit. Sometimes food companies are tricky and add sugar or preservatives. What do you see? Is it bigger or smaller? How does it feel? What do you smell? Let's taste it. What is the texture? What is the taste?
- The last piece of fruit is freeze-dried. What do you see? How does it feel? What do you smell? Let's taste it. What is its texture? How does it taste? Let's compare them. Do they look the same or different? Do they smell the same? Do they feel different? Which is healthiest? Why?

RAISINS AND GRAPES

While a raisin may look very different from a grape, they are actually the same fruit. A raisin is simply a dried grape. Even though they are the same fruit, the raisin and the grape have different health components. When fruits are dried, their contents become more concentrated. The raisin has more antioxidants, calories, and sugar.

Materials

- Red raisins
- Grapes

Benefits

Mindful eating with raisins and grapes helps children focus on internal cues, pay attention to what they're eating, and listen to what their bodies are telling them.

What to Say

- I'm going to place a grape in your hand. Look at the grape as if you have never seen it before. What do you see? What is the shape? Color? Now rub your finger across it. What do you feel? Close your eyes. Bring the grape up to your nose. What do you smell? What does it remind you of? Put the grape in your mouth. Chew slowly. What do you taste?
- Now let's be mindful with our raisin. Repeat the same process with the raisin. How are the grape and raisin similar? How are they different?

Mindfulness Variation

Try using green grapes and golden raisins, too, for a different taste challenge. You can also have children close their eyes and see if they can taste which raisin or grape is which color.

APPLESAUCE APPETIZERS

Drinking applesauce through a straw is hard work, but kids love it. (Kids love blowing a few bubbles in the applesauce, as well.) Mix in different types of straws, such as curly straws or wider straws, and have your child notice which straw is easiest to drink from.

Materials

- Pureed organic applesauce
- Thick straws, skinny straws, curly straws
- Paper cup

Benefits

Eating applesauce through a straw is great for oral motor development, which can improve speech skills. Sucking is calming and can be organizing to the brain and nervous system. Blowing in the applesauce is great for the respiratory system.

What to Say

- Our mindful snack today is applesauce, but there is a catch. We are going to eat our applesauce through these three straws.
- As you suck in your applesauce, notice which straw makes you work harder. What does it feel like to suck the applesauce? What do you smell? Remember to sip slowly. There is no rush. Let's try the next straw. Is it different from the first? What do you notice? Here's the last one, stay mindful. What do you notice?
- Let's see what happens when we blow into the straw. What did you notice?

BLACKOUT

We've established that it is pretty important to use your senses when you are being mindful, but what happens if we take one sense away? Sometimes when you take one sense away, the other senses become heightened. It also makes the exercise novel, which engages the brain. Blackout involves eating mindfully with our eyes closed.

Materials

- Two small squares of organic dark chocolate

Benefits

Eating mindfully, with eyes closed, helps children slow down while eating and reduces mindless eating. This fun exercise also leads to more enjoyment of the mindful snack and an inner awareness.

What to Say

- We are going to pretend there is a blackout and mindfully eat a snack with our eyes shut. Sit up tall in Easy Seated Pose. Close your eyes. Hold out your hand with your palm facing up. I am going to put something in your hand. Don't open your eyes. What do you feel? Is it warm, cold? Is it heavy, light? What is the texture? Bring it up to your nose. Take in a deep breath. What do you smell? Is it bitter or sweet? Shake it by your ear. Does it make a sound?
- Keeping your eyes closed, put it on your tongue. Notice what you taste before biting down. Begin to chew slowly. How does the food taste? What is your reaction to this food?
- Keeping your eyes closed, let's eat one more piece. Hold out your hand. Slowly, put this in your mouth and eat it mindfully. What did you notice when eating with your eyes shut? How is it different from eating with your eyes open?

FRUIT CATERPILLAR

Kids are more apt to eat healthy when they make their own snack. Kids love making animal art out of food. For extra fun read the book *The Very Hungry Caterpillar* before you make the caterpillar. Younger kids might need a little help with the skewer.

Materials

- Grapes
- Strawberries
- White chocolate chips
- Pretzel sticks
- Blueberries
- Carrots (matchstick)
- Wooden skewer

Benefits

The Fruit Caterpillar is loaded with healthy fruits that are rich with antioxidants, vitamins, and minerals. Placing the fruit on the skewer is great for developing eye-hand coordination and fine motor skills.

What to Say

- We are going to make a Fruit Caterpillar by putting the following ingredients on this long stick, called a skewer. Let's start with the caterpillar body. Put these six grapes on the skewer to make the body. How do the grapes feel? What color are they? Then place the strawberry at the top for the head. How does the strawberry feel? What does it look like?
- Next, let's push the white chocolate chips into the top of the strawberry for the eyes. Now let's give our caterpillar antennae. Bring the pretzel up to your nose. What do you smell? Press two pretzel sticks into the strawberry for the antennae, then place a blueberry on top of each pretzel stick.
- Where should we place the carrot sticks? Right alongside the grapes, to make legs. What did you notice while you were making the caterpillar? Were you being mindful while making it? How so?

CHOP-CHOP BREATHE

Teaching your child to use chopsticks is a great learning experience. Using chopsticks forces children to slow down, eat deliberately, and take smaller portions of food. Hmmm...sounds a lot like mindful eating.

Materials

- Kid's chopsticks

Benefits

Chopsticks teach children patience and appreciation for the food they are eating. Chopsticks also encourage eating slowly, which is good for digestion.

What to Say

- We are going to try a new style of eating fruit—with chopsticks! Remember, to learn a new skill, we have to practice six times, and some skills take even more time, so it's okay if it feels uncomfortable at first. Let's slowly pick up our first piece of fruit. What do you see? Can you bring it up to your nose without dropping it?
- Take a deep breath in. What do you smell? Let's see if we can make it to our mouths. Great focus! What do you taste? Let's keep mindfully using our chopsticks to eat our snack.

SALAD BAR

Salads aren't just for grown-ups! Salads are a great way for children to get their daily amounts of fruits and vegetables and to learn about healthy eating. Set out all the ingredients. Let your child choose a little bit of this and a little bit of that. Encourage him to make it a colorful salad because deep colors mean that it is a nutritious meal. Make a rainbow in every bowl!

Materials

- Spinach
- Cherry tomatoes
- Shredded carrots
- Sliced peppers (orange, yellow, red)
- Sliced avocado
- Shredded cheese
- Mandarin oranges
- Edamame
- Quinoa
- Organic dressing
- Bowls
- Serving spoons and forks
- Ambient music

Benefits

Salad Bar is a fun way to educate your child in making healthy food choices. The phytonutrients in salads boost the immune system, keeping your little one healthy. Salads contain healthy carbohydrates that fill children up and reduce overeating.

What to Say

- We are going to make our own salads. I'm sure you know that eating a variety of fruits and vegetables is healthy for our brains and bodies, but did you know that salads aren't just for grown-ups?
- I'm going to play some music and we are going to mindfully make our salads. This means we are going to pay attention with our senses as we make and eat our salads. We aren't going to talk. Instead we are going to notice what we see, hear, smell, feel, and taste. We will eat our salads slowly, noticing each bite. Notice when you start to feel full. Ready? Go.

MEALTIME MINDFULNESS

Mealtime Mindfulness is taking a moment before you eat to thank those who have contributed to the meal. Being mindful at mealtime also means reducing distractions—that means turning off or putting away electronic devices, such as TVs and phones. Instead of filling your child's plate full of food, offer only the amount you think she can eat. There is always the opportunity to refill a plate.

Benefits

Thanking others, such as thanking the farmers for the fruits and vegetables, teaches your child to be grateful for the food she is about to eat. It also brings awareness to where the food came from. Reducing distractions allows families to notice and appreciate each other and the meal.

What to Say

- We are going to eat our meal mindfully. This means we are going to turn off all electronic devices, such as the TV, iPad, phones, and computers. What sounds do you notice once these devices are off?
- Before we begin eating, let's thank the farmers who grew our fruits and vegetables. Thank you, farmers, for all your hard work planting, growing, picking, and selling these wonderful fruits and vegetables so we can have healthy food to eat.
- Let's quietly eat our meal, noticing each bite, smell, and sound while we eat. Ready? Begin.

Mindful Eating Activities and Games

Practicing eating mindfully, as we did in the previous section, is a great hands-on way to rethink what you put in your mouth. But there are other ways to teach kids about mindful eating, like arts and crafts and games! The next section covers those types of activities.

FAKE FOOD

Kids are easily drawn to certain products because of their brightly colored packaging, favorite characters, and prizes hidden inside...yet those products often seem to be the least healthy options! It is hard for children to understand that some products don't actually contain much, if any, real food. This activity introduces children to the concept that not all food is real.

Materials

- Grocery store coupon flyers
- Poster board
- Scissors
- Glue

Benefits

Fake Food teaches children about making healthy food choices. The cutting and gluing helps with fine motor development. This activity also teaches children how to categorize.

What to Say

- Did you know that some of the foods we eat are not real? These foods are instead made from chemicals and are not healthy to eat. Sometimes it is difficult to figure out what is real and good for us and what is not.
- We are going make a poster board that shows us which foods are real and which ones are fake. Fake food usually comes in packages, is an unusual or bright color like turquoise or yellowy orange, and has a list of ingredients that

you don't recognize. Many unhealthy choices feature characters on the box, and they are often made with something called high-fructose corn syrup, which is an unhealthy type of sugar.

- Foods that are real grow in the ground or on trees. They are usually sold in stores exactly as they came from nature.
- Look through these magazines and find foods that are real and foods that are fake. Cut them out. We will glue them on our poster board under the labels "Real" and "Fake."

Mindfulness Challenge

For older children, make a borderline category and have them find items that have misleading messages, such as "contains fruit" or "100% whole wheat," and discuss whether they are real foods.

FRUIT AND VEGGIE MONSTER

This is an activity best suited for preschoolers. Cut a large hole in a box to make a giant mouth. Draw a friendly monster face on it. Maybe even add some blue or purple material to make his face furry. Have your child hold pieces of fruit mindfully and throw each piece of pretend food into the Fruit and Veggie Monster's mouth. Make sure you discuss the health benefits of each fruit before you throw it. For a fun twist, feed the Fruit and Veggie Monster an ice cream cone or unhealthy food and have him spit it out right away.

Materials

- Large box
- Plastic food

Benefits

The Fruit and Veggie Monster improves eye-hand coordination. It teaches children to slow down and notice what they are eating with their senses, which builds mindful awareness. It is a fun way to build language skills and learn about the foods we eat.

What to Say

- This is our friend, the Fruit and Veggie Monster. He loves fruit, vegetables, healthy foods, and mindful eating. Unhealthy foods and mindless eating make his tummy hurt.
- Look in your basket of food. Which items will the monster like the best? You picked a carrot, an orange, and a banana. Good choices! Let's start with the orange. Sit up tall. Take a deep breath in. Let it out. What does it look like? How does it feel? How is an orange healthy? That's right, it has lots of vitamin C.
- Go ahead and gently throw it in the Fruit and Veggie Monster's mouth. Yay! He liked it. Is the carrot a fruit or vegetable? Right, a vegetable. What does the carrot look like? How does it feel? Does it make a sound? How are carrots healthy? They are good for your eyes! Okay, let's see if he likes it.
- Let's try another food now. Watch out, though, if it's not healthy and we didn't practice mindfulness, he may spit it out!

SAVVY SHOPPER

The supermarket is a great educational classroom—you might as well use it when you have your kids with you at the store. If time and resources allow, kids love picking their own foods and pushing their own little carts! The perimeter of the grocery store is where the healthy foods are housed. The middle of the store is filled with processed junk foods. This is an important lesson to teach children early in life.

Benefits

Children will learn the health benefits of produce while exploring the grocery store. Eating healthy foods is vital for your child's brain and body. Allowing your child to pick his own food provides a sense of pride, and makes him want to eat the healthy foods he has picked. For all children, using their senses improves focus on the tasks and engages mindful awareness.

What to Say

- We are going shopping. I am going to give you your own cart. Remember, we want to do as much of our shopping as we can on the edges of the grocery store, not the middle aisles.
- Let's start in the fruit and veggie section. Can you pick out one blue, two red, three yellow, and two orange foods that you would like to eat? Remember to smell, feel, and really look at each food you pick. Great mindfulness! Colorful berries and veggies are good for our brains and bodies.
- Now let's find some green foods. Can you find three green foods you would like to eat this week? Fantastic, these are perfect green foods that are good for you.

Mindfulness Challenge

For older children, have them find two healthy food items that are in the middle of the store. This will require some mindful detective work when they are looking at the ingredients lists on the foods.

Brain Challenge

Have older children point out two kinds of the same food from an aisle (for example, cereal aisle or juice section), one not healthy and the other a healthier option.

HAPPIER MEAL

Kids love Happy Meals from McDonald's; however, *happy* does not mean *healthy*. This activity provides the fun of McDonald's, but with healthier choices. Eating a healthy Happier Meal requires a change in the way your child thinks about food.

Materials

- Paper bag
- Markers
- Stickers
- Small prize such as a bottle of bubble solution
- Apple slices
- Small bottled water
- Healthy chicken nuggets (made with organic chicken, sea salt, organic egg, organic whole wheat bread crumbs)

Benefits

Happier Meal enhances fine motor skills. It is a fun way to practice mindful awareness. Adding a mindful prize like a small bottle of bubble solution engages children in deep breathing, which is calming. Mindful eating teaches children to notice how their body feels and what it needs instead of mindlessly munching when they are bored or watching TV.

What to Say

- We are going to make our own Happier Meal. First, let's decorate our Happier Meal sack. Remember it is a "happier" meal, so we want to put happy words and faces on it. Great.
- Next, let's put our meal in it.
- Let's sit up tall in Easy Seated Pose and have a picnic with our Happier Meals. Since this is a "happier" meal, we will try to only engage in happy talk. Use kind words and talk about the good things that are happening around us. Take a deep breath in. Let it out. What do you see? How does the bag feel? What do you smell? Let's open it and start to eat our Happier Meal!

YOGURT SLIME

Homemade slime is typically made out of borax, glue, and other ingredients that you don't want children ingesting. This easy mindfulness activity only calls for yogurt (without the fruit) and cornstarch, making it an easy and healthy alternative. Yogurt Slime is squishy, soft, and smells good, making it a fun mindful eating activity for children of all ages.

Materials

- 1 cup strawberry yogurt
- ¾ cup cornstarch

Benefits

Yogurt slime improves tactile discrimination, body awareness, and creative exploration. Drawing and playing with Yogurt Slime helps children build the skills necessary to move the eyes, hands, and body together. Playing with different textures makes the brain calmer and more organized.

What to Say

- We are going to make Yogurt Slime. Pour strawberry yogurt and cornstarch into this mixing bowl. Mix it together with your hands and then begin to play with it until it is no longer sticky and you are able to roll it into a ball. If it is too dry, add a little bit more yogurt, and if it is too sticky, add a little bit more cornstarch.
- Now that we have the slime made just right, we will practice mindfulness. Sit up tall. Take a deep Elevator Breath (Chapter 3). Let it out. Close your eyes. Take a moment to notice how the slime feels in your hands with your senses. Is it heavy or light? Warm or cool? Smooth or bumpy? What do you notice about the shape? Bring your slime up to your nose. What does it smell like? Ah...smells delicious.
- Open your eyes. What do you see? Not all slime can be tasted, but this slime is different. This slime is made of yogurt, which is good for us. Let's taste a small bite. Remember, pay attention to what is happening in your mouth. What did the slime taste like?

MANDALA DOUGH

Mandala is the Sanskrit word for "circle." It represents being united, connected, and whole. Mandala Dough is a way to involve the senses and mindfulness in an art activity by making your own mandala. The dough can be formed into a large circle to frame the mandala and then filled in with lines, hearts, circles, or any shapes your child's mind imagines. This is a quiet activity, so limit talking and play ambient music to enhance the mindfulness state.

This activity can be done in a group or one-on-one. It is appropriate for all ages. However, check for allergies. Substitutions, such as almond butter, may need to be made. If you are doing this at home, involve your child in making the dough. If this is being done in a group setting, make the dough beforehand and place it in a plastic container until you are ready to use it. To make the dough, simply mix the honey, peanut butter, and dried milk thoroughly in a bowl. It should feel like dough—not too dry or sticky. Keep adding ingredients until you reach the right consistency.

Materials

- Mandala designs, printed out
- 2 cups honey
- 2 cups peanut butter
- 4 cups nonfat dried milk
- Baking sheet
- NOTE: Allergies may require substitutions

Benefits

Making mandalas promotes focus, concentration, and an overall meditative state, which helps children feel calm and relaxed. Playing with Play-Doh tends to be calming due to the proprioceptive input it provides hands. Play-Doh also strengthens hands and fingers, which prepares hands for school tasks, such as handwriting.

What to Say

- Let's wash our hands. It's mandala time! *Mandala* is a word from the yoga language than means "circle." It means we are united or connected. I'm going to put a few mandala designs on the table. You can choose one as an example to follow or create your own.
- Let's begin by siting up tall in Easy Seated Pose and taking a couple of deep Balloon Breaths to prepare our minds and bodies for creativity. Pick up a piece of the dough. What does it smell like? Can you identify what it is made of? Does the dough make a sound? What does it feel like? Slimy or rough? Heavy or light?
- Let's begin. First, make a big circle to frame our mandala. How can we make it into a circle? Correct, we need to roll it! Now that we have our outline, you can roll, pat, and shape your dough into your very own mandala.

MARSHMALLOW CHALLENGE

This mindfulness activity involves both building and creativity—a great mix for kids! Children will build a tower out of only marshmallows and spaghetti. The biggest problem with this challenge is stopping children from eating their creations.

Materials

- One package of uncooked organic spaghetti
- Two packages of organic marshmallows

Benefits

Marshmallow Challenge enhances creativity and problem-solving. Creative play has significant benefits for children's overall well-being. Creative experiences foster emotional growth in children by supporting new ways of thinking.

What to Say

- We are going to make buildings out of marshmallows and spaghetti noodles. Let's start by building pyramids with four marshmallows on the bottom.
- Notice your marshmallows. How do the marshmallows feel? What do they smell like?
- What do the spaghetti noodles feel and smell like?
- How about making a tower? The key to building a tall tower is making a strong, wide base. Let's use two spaghetti noodles between marshmallows to make it extra strong. Remember to push the spaghetti deep into the marshmallows. Let's keep building. What should we do next?

Brain Challenge

Ask the children, "Can your tower hold an egg on top? How is this possible? Yes, by building a nest with the short spaghetti pieces in the marshmallow."

LEPRECHAUN GOLD

If your children like the idea of hunting for buried treasure, they will love this mindful eating activity. The Jell-O rainbow needs to be made the day before you introduce the activity. Hide the gold coins in the rainbow and let the messy fun begin.

Materials

- 3–6 (3-ounce) packages of Jell-O (in rainbow colors)
- 1 cup boiling water per Jell-O package
- ⅔ cup vanilla yogurt per Jell-O package
- ⅔ cup cold water per Jell-O package
- 9" x 13" baking dish
- Several chocolate gold coins

Benefits

This multisensory activity provides tactile input and mindful awareness. It also helps children improve their fine motor skills and color recognition, and encourages exploratory play.

How to Make Rainbow Jell-O

- Choose one color of Jell-O to start with. Add 1 cup of boiling water to the Jell-O powder. Stir until Jell-O is dissolved.
- After dissolved, split liquid into two bowls.
- Whisk ⅔ cup yogurt into one bowl, stirring until smooth.
- Add ⅔ cup cold water to the other bowl and whisk for 20 seconds.
- Pour the yogurt mixture into a 9" x 13" pan. Put in freezer for 15 minutes or until the Jell-O has set.
- Push gold coins into the yogurt layer.
- Pour water mixture slowly over yogurt mixture and let solidify in fridge for at least 45 minutes or put it in the freezer for 15 minutes.
- Repeat process for the rest of the Jell-O packages. Make as many layers as you like.

What to Say

- Did you know leprechauns like to hide their gold at the end of a rainbow? We are going to search for leprechaun gold.
- Before we dig for our gold, let's explore our rainbow mindfully, using all of our senses. What do you see? What are the different colors? How many colors are there?

- Now for the fun part—dig in with your hands! How does the rainbow feel? Is it hot or cold? Bring a chunk of it up to your nose. What do you smell? Let's taste it. What is the texture? What is the taste? Is it sweet or sour? Do the different colors taste the same or different?
- Finally, let's search for the leprechaun gold! When you find a piece, mindfully unwrap it and take a bite.

MINDFUL EATING IN LITERATURE

Books are a wonderful way to introduce peaceful living concepts to children. There are some delightful children's books with accompanying mindful eating actitivities to encourage children to slow down, eat mindfully, and try new foods.

MINDFUL DINOSAURS

What could be a better way to introduce mindful eating to children than through a hilarious story about dinosaurs? Read aloud the book *How Do Dinosaurs Eat Their Food?* At the end of each page, discuss whether the dinosaur was eating mindfully or mindlessly. If you have a dry erase board, make two columns, labeled Mindful and Mindless. List the dinosaurs and their eating habits under each category. At the end of the story reflect on the dinosaurs' eating habits.

Materials

- Book, *How Do Dinosaurs Eat Their Food?* by Jane Yolen

Benefits

Books engage young children and hidden messages are sometimes more powerful and memorable than direct teaching moments. Children will learn the difference between mindful and mindless behaviors indirectly through the dinosaurs.

What to Say

- Sit up tall in Easy Seated Pose. We are going to read a book on how dinosaurs eat their food. Eating mindfully is when we pay attention to our food and our manners.
- We are going to pay careful attention to whether the different dinosaurs are being mindful or mindless and write them on this chart.

CHAPTER 6

Mindful Activities for Focus

For children to practice mindfulness, they must slow down, just be, and focus on one thing at a time—but that can be tough to do in today's world! Focusing your attention on what is happening in the moment is part of being mindful. Mindfulness also involves paying attention with the senses and keeping an open mind about situations until you have reflected on them (being nonjudgmental).

A great way for children to begin to pay attention is to focus on their own bodies. Activities that introduce noticing the breath and thoughts, and paying attention to how the body feels during and after movement and stillness, will help children become more skillful at being mindful and practicing focused awareness. When children are mindfully aware of themselves and their environment, new details are revealed to them, which can transform the experience itself. Small objects such as coins, insects, hands, and paper take on new meaning. When children unplug and experience the art of paying attention on purpose, they reap the benefits of the mindfulness activities—they enjoy being present, aware, and in the moment, which are important life skills. The simple and fun mindfulness exercises in this chapter are designed to specifically help children focus on the present moment, while improving mindful awareness and memory, as well.

FIBER OPTIC FOCUS

Practicing focus means that you notice when your mind is distracted, catch it, and bring it back to whatever you are trying to focus on. Fiber Optic Focus involves having your child focus his attention on an engaging visual object, encouraging him to notice when his mind starts to wander, and having him bring his attention back to focusing on the object. This activity requires the use of a fiber optic lamp, which can be bought inexpensively online.

Materials

- Vibrating fiber optic light or fiber optic light

Benefits

Having children notice when their minds wander and practice bringing it back helps them to improve attention. The longer children are able to focus on an object, the more their mindfulness will increase. The fiber optic strings also provide calming tactile and visual input.

What to Say

- Choose a comfortable position. Take a few deep breaths to settle in. Let's practice Fiber Optic Focus! Begin to watch the fiber optic lamp. Watch the strings swirl and reflect the changing colors. Let it fill up your gaze and mind. Tune everything else out.
- When your mind starts to wander, that's okay! Just notice it, and bring your attention back to the lamp. Close your eyes and try to keep the object you have been gazing at fixed in your mind. Take a few deep breaths, and when you are ready open your eyes. Notice how you feel.

STARFISH HANDS

This is a short hand meditation that can be done anywhere. Children begin by focusing on their breath while tracing their Starfish Hands (fingers spread wide). Then their starfish becomes scared and tightens up into a tight ball. By using the power of breathing, the starfish is able to relax again.

Benefits

Starfish Hands is calming and relaxing. It encourages kids to recognize their emotions and promotes focus, concentration, and attention. This activity begins to teach body and mindful awareness.

What to Say

- Let's imagine our hands are starfish. Hold one hand up and spread your fingers out—that's starfish position. Let's gently trace up and down each finger with the pointer finger of your other hand, while focusing on breathing in and out through your nose.
- Now let's make a starfish with your other hand. Gently and slowly trace this starfish. Remember to breathe. Ah, now your starfish is nice and relaxed.
- Now imagine that a giant shark is approaching and your starfish becomes scared. Interlace your fingers and squeeze your hands tightly for ten seconds. Release them. Now focus on how your hands feel. What do you notice? Breathe in and out through your nose. Stay focused on the feeling in your hands for as long as you can or until that feeling goes away. When the tight feeling is gone, begin to trace your starfish one more time. How do you feel?

POP QUIZ

Read a short story—for example, *Rotten Ralph*—and then infuse it with yoga poses, breath work, and mindfulness. At the end of the story, give your child a "pop quiz" on the content. Have her show you the yoga poses, breath work, and mindfulness activities she remembers, as she explains what happened in the story. Children love Rotten Ralph because he is always misbehaving and getting into mischief. Rotten Ralph tries to overcome his rottenness and redeem himself, but no matter what, his family still loves him. For inspiration, here is a list of ideas to incorporate into Rotten Ralph:

- Dancer Pose: Ralph makes fun of Sarah dancing (Chapter 2).
- Tree Pose: Grow your branches (arms) and then have one arm drop down when Ralph saws off the tree branch (Chapter 2).
- Elevator Breath: Lie on your back the same way Ralph does when he takes a bite out of all of the cookies (Chapter 3).
- Balloon Breath: Ralph's soap bubbles (Chapter 3).
- Yoga Bicycles: Ralph smashes into the cake with his bike (Chapter 2).
- Down Dog Pose: Ralph is sitting next to the Dog at the Circus. Don't forget to bark and stomp your feet (Chapter 2)!
- Lion's Pose and Lion's Breath: Ralph floats over the Lion's cage (Chapter 3).
- Monkey Pose: Ralph is left at the Circus (Chapter 2).
- Camel Pose: Ralph waters the camels (Chapter 2).
- Cobra Pose: There is a blue snake slithering by Ralph's cage (Chapter 2).
- Cross Crawls: Ralph runs away from the Circus (Chapter 2).
- Child's Pose: Mice are nibbling on Ralph's toes (Chapter 2).
- Fish Pose: Ralph is cold and sad and looking in the trash, and there is a dead fish on the ground (Chapter 2).
- Spread your arms wide and then give yourself a great big hug: Sarah finds Ralph.

- Mummy Pose with Counting Breaths: Ralph rides home in his wagon (Chapters 2 and 3).
- Butterfly Breath: Ralph arrives home (Chapter 3).

Materials

- *Rotten Ralph* by Jack Gantos

Benefits

Pop Quiz enhances creativity, focus, and attention. Pop Quiz builds working memory and concentration, development of logic, and mindfulness. It promotes yoga pose practice and review.

What to Say

- We are going to read a story about Rotten Ralph. Rotten Ralph is always misbehaving and sometimes it is hard for him to stay out of trouble. As we read the story we will engage in mindfulness and movement activities. Sit up tall in Easy Seated Pose. Ready? Let's begin.

Brain Challenge

After children have listened to the story, have them take it a step further by asking them what they think happened after the book ends. Have your child show you what happened next with movement, breath, and mindfulness.

POLAROID

A Polaroid camera takes a picture that instantly prints out. This Polaroid activity involves taking a mental snapshot and remembering the order objects are placed in. For this activity, any small objects may be used, but it may be more engaging if you incorporate things your child enjoys. For example, if your child likes to play with cars, use small toy cars that are different colors, shapes, or models. If your child loves the ocean, use seashells. Try to incorporate objects that will spark her interest and engagement.

Materials

- Six small toys or objects
- Small blanket or towel

Benefits

Polaroid can improve visual working memory and enhance executive functioning skills and mindful awareness. It is a simple activity to build focus and attention while playing into your child's personal interests.

What to Say

- I'm going to set out four objects—you probably recognize them! Look at the items for five seconds, and try to remember what order they are in.
- Now I'm going to put a blanket over the items and scramble them up. Your job is to put them back in the order they were in originally. Ready?
- Wow! That was fantastic remembering. I think you need a bit more of a challenge. Now I'm going to ask you to remember six items. Here we go!

Brain Challenge

For younger children, use only two objects that are distinctly different. For older children, start with four objects that are similar and continue to add more objects with each turn until your child starts to have trouble remembering. This will help him build his visual memory skills.

MINDFUL MUSIC

Play your child's favorite song. Have her listen to it mindfully while engaging in Elevator Breaths (Chapter 3). Instruct her to pay attention to how that music makes her feel. Then ask her to draw a picture of how the music makes her feel. Afterward, discuss the experience with your child.

Materials

- Colored pencils or markers
- Paper

Benefits

Mindful Music encourages mindful awareness and builds listening skills and focus. Listening to a song you enjoy can be uplifting and shift a negative perspective to a positive one.

What to Say

- I'm going to play your favorite song. Listen to it carefully and mindfully. Pay close attention to how the music makes you feel. What emotions does it bring out? What does it remind you of? What memories do you have of this song?
- Let's draw a picture of how the song makes you feel and what it reminds you of. Great picture!

FIND IT

Find It is a hidden adventure game. Find It can be purchased online or you and your child can make the game together to incorporate only the items you want in it. To make a homemade Find It game, place small objects (small erasers shaped like objects work well) in a large jar, fill it with rice, and shut the lid. Once you have your Find It game, make a code for the items that is mindfulness-based. For inspiration, here is a list of items you could include:

- Balloon: If you or your child finds the balloon, take three Balloon Breaths (Chapter 3).
- Snake: If you or your child finds the snake, pretend to be a cobra with Cobra Pose for three breaths (Chapter 2).
- Monkey: If you or your child finds the monkey, pretend to be a monkey with Monkey Pose for three breaths (Chapter 2).
- Dog: If you or your child finds the dog, do Down Dog Pose for three breaths (Chapter 2).
- Rainbow: If you or your child finds a rainbow, look around the room and find all the colors of the rainbow.
- Unicorn: If you or your child finds the unicorn, pretend to be a unicorn for three breaths.
- Musical Note: Play an ambient music song filled with nature sounds. Listen carefully and name three nature sounds you hear.
- Kindness Coin: Make a kind wish for a friend, family member, and someone who bothers you.
- Lotus Flower: Make the Lotus Mudra (Chapter 7) with your hands and hold for three breaths.

Materials

- Plastic or glass jar with a wide mouth
- Rice
- Small toy objects (bee, balloon, snake, monkey, musical note, dog, rainbow, unicorn, Kindness Coin)

Benefits

Find It boosts creativity and mindfulness. This activity enhances focus, visual recognition skills, and concentration. Find It will help your child remember and practice yoga poses, mindfulness exercises, and breath work.

What to Say

- Let's play Find It! In this jar, I've hidden ten objects. Your job is to find the items by moving the jar slowly and carefully in your hands. Once you have found an item, we will do the mindfulness activity associated with the item. Then we will cross it off our list and look for the other items. Remember to use your mindfulness skills of paying attention on purpose to find the items!

Mindfulness Variation

For older children, hide Yoga Joes in the rice. Color the rice to match the Yoga Joes (they come in various colors) and when your child finds the Joe, have her hold that pose for ten breaths. This variation will build strength, flexibility, and focus.

TOEGA

Toega or Toe Yoga is yoga for your child's toes. Toega creates happy, healthy movement in your child's feet. This activity requires pom-poms and a plastic container. Scatter pom-poms on the ground and have your child pick them up using only his toes. Have him switch feet and mindfully notice if there is a difference in dexterity between his feet. Also, have him notice which size of pom-pom is easier to pick up. After the activity, discuss the experience with your child.

Materials

- Pom-poms of various sizes
- Small plastic bowl

Benefits

Toega improves focus, concentration, and attention while increasing strength and flexibility in the toes and feet.

What to Say

- We are going to play Toega, which is yoga for your toes. Pick up the pom-poms with your toes and place them in the bucket. Let's use our right foot first. Notice how the pom-poms feel in your toes.
- Now let's try our left foot. Did you notice a difference between your feet? Can you pick up pom-poms with both feet at the same time? Great coordination! Which size of pom-poms was easier or harder to pick up?

Mindfulness Variation

Add a yoga hammock. Sitting in a yoga hammock adds movement, which requires extra focus and coordination to pick up pom-poms and put them in a bucket with your toes. Make it extra challenging by spreading the pom-poms out so children have to swing and spin to pick them up.

Brain Challenge

Tell the children, "Stretch your toes out wide." Then put crayons between each of their toes. Put poster boards underneath their feet and have them start to draw with their feet. Can they print their name?

ZEN GARDEN

Zen gardens use rocks, sand, and elements of nature to create a peaceful place. These tiny manmade landscapes can serve as a focal point while meditating. While you can easily order a kit online, it's a lot more fun and cost effective to find the elements in your own home or yard and create your child's own mini meditation paradise.

Materials

- Shoebox lid or small shallow dish
- Sand
- Water
- Tea light holder
- Small rocks, seashells, and/or polished rocks
- Moss
- Comb, fork, twigs, or mini rake
- Small plastic bridge or piece of cardboard

Benefits

Building a Zen Garden is a relaxing way to explore natural materials and build concentration. It is a fun, quiet activity for the entire family. Zen Garden allows children to use their creativity, which boosts imagination and cognitive development.

What to Say

- We are going to make a Zen Garden. *Zen* means "relaxed," or not worrying about things you can't change. So a Zen Garden is a garden that helps you relax and reduces your worries.
- Let's go for a walk and find some rocks to represent mountains for our garden. Maybe we can find some plants as well. Perfect.
- Now we'll make the garden. First, let's pour the sand in the bottom of our garden. Place the rocks in the sand. In a traditional zen garden, the rocks are placed in the four corners, but you can place them wherever you want.

- Put the empty tea light holder in the sand. Let's fill it up with water. Should we place the bridge over the water?
- Use your mini rake to make patterns in the sand. We can also make tracks in the sand with our fingers and patterns with the bark, seashells, stones, and moss. When we are done we can smooth it out and start again. As you make patterns, breathe in and out slowly through your nose. Notice how the garden smells, feels, looks, and sounds. After you're done, notice how you feel.

BE HERE NOW

Be Here Now is a short mindfulness activity that can be used to help calm a busy mind and bring your child's awareness to the present moment. Children will notice things they are experiencing with their senses: things they can see, touch, hear, smell, and taste. The examples shown in this exercise are courtesy of Lindsey Lieneck of Yogapeutics.

Benefits

Be Here Now builds mindful awareness and reflection skills.

What to Say

- Lie in a comfortable position, such as Mummy Pose (Chapter 2). Close your eyes and start to engage in Elevator Breath (Chapter 3). We are going to practice being in the now, which means we notice what is happening around and within us with our senses. Remember to just notice, not to judge as "good" or "bad." Take three more deep Elevator Breaths, then open your eyes. Here are some activity examples to practice Be Here Now:
    - Notice five objects you can see. Look around and notice five things that you normally don't pay attention to, such as a shadow, a plant, or a crack in the ceiling.
    - Notice four objects you can hear. Listen carefully. Note four things that you can hear right now. This could be the heater, a bird singing, or cars driving past.
    - Notice three objects you can feel. Bring your attention to something you can feel, like the ground beneath you, the warm air, or the cuff of your sleeve touching your wrist.
    - Notice two objects you can smell. Take a deep breath in. Pay attention to what you smell. Maybe you smell an essential oil or the soap that is on your hands. Just notice what you smell.
    - Here is a tricky one. Notice one object that you can taste. Notice the taste in your mouth. If there is nothing to taste, chew a piece of gum or take a sip of water. Or just notice what "nothing" tastes like!

WEATHER REPORT

Weather Report allows children to be their own meterologist. Your child will take a moment to notice and reflect on how he feels on the inside, which is his personal weather. This simple activity helps children begin to notice how they are feeling and what their bodies need in order to feel happy and calm.

Materials

- Paper
- Colored pencils

Benefits

Weather Report teaches children to notice how they are feeling, recognize emotions, and self-regulate. It promotes mindful awareness, focus, concentration, and inner peace.

What to Say

- Let's make a Weather Report. Sit in Easy Seated Pose (Chapter 2). Close your eyes. Pretend you are a weather station and your emotions are the weather.
- Notice how you are feeling. What is your inner weather? Are you happy and relaxed like a warm summer day? Or do you feel tense and stressed like a stormy day? Maybe it's sunny, but you still feel restless and fidgety and need to move, so there is a lot of wind in your Weather Report. Take five deep Balloon Breaths (Chapter 3). Notice what is going on inside you. Let's draw our Weather Report.

Mindful Games for Focus

Playing games is not only fun, it is how children learn. The right game can boost your child's visual and auditory attention skills. These mindful focus games don't take much time and kids love playing them!

WALK THROUGH THE FOREST

Walk Through the Forest is a group activity for children of all ages. Each child will be in Tree Pose (Chapter 2), forming a forest. One child will walk through the forest, while the Trees try to remain balanced. Once a Tree loses her balance, that Tree starts to walk through the forest, too, until there is only one focused Tree remaining.

Benefits

Balancing poses such as Tree Pose improve concentration and teach perseverance. A Walk Through the Forest increases flexibility, focus, and strength.

What to Say

- I need one volunteer. Great, you will walk through the forest. Everyone else will be a Tree. My volunteer is going to walk through the forest, being careful not to touch the Trees. Everyone else is going to hold Tree Pose as long as possible. Be mindful of the forest and don't touch the Trees.
- Tree Pose is hard to stay in! Once you fall out of the pose, you will walk through the remaining forest until there is only one Tree left standing. Look at all these wonderful Trees standing tall!
- That was fantastic focus. Let's do it one more time, but on your other leg!

Mindfulness Variation

If the forest is very solid and the Trees are not falling down, ask the Trees to close their eyes and sway their branches back and forth. This will require more focus and will be more challenging for the children.

CREATE A SUN DANCE

Sun Salutations in yoga are sometimes referred to as Sun Dances in children's classes. Creating a Sun Dance is a simple and fun way to enhance focus and get your child moving. This mindfulness activity has children creating their own Sun Salutation sequence. This activity works best with a group of children who are six years old and up.

Benefits

Sun Dance improves creativity and working memory because it reviews poses and breathing activities. It gives children a chance to teach or lead an activity, which boosts adaptive skills, such as self-esteem and leadership.

What to Say

- Let's do "Hello, Sunshine" (Chapter 2) a couple of times.
- Did you notice that "Hello, Sunshine" is several poses put together to make a flow? Let's create our own flow or Sun Salutation. Each of you is going to add a pose or mindful breathing exercise to the Sun Salutation. Let's go in a line. Remember the order the poses go in. Each of you will take turns creating a pose. The next child in line mirrors the first pose and adds a pose to the dance. This continues until everyone has added two poses to the Sun Salutation.
- Now that we have created the flow, we will practice moving through our special Sun Salutation.

MINDFUL COINS AND STICKS

Mindful Coins and Sticks is a visual focus activity for children eight years old and older. This activity will require your child's full attention. Each child will be given a coin and a stick. Other objects can be used, so long as they look similar, yet have some characteristic that will distinguish each one. For example, quarters may look the same, but when you mindfully observe the coins you'll notice that the year may be different. Have each child examine their coin mindfully, then place it in a basket. Mix up the coins and then ask children to find their own coins. Repeat the exercise with the sticks. After the exercise, discuss the experience with the group. For this activity, you might ask them, "How did you find your coin and stick?" "How was finding the coin different from finding the stick?" "Did you find it challenging to focus on your coin or stick?" "What are some tools we can use to help us focus?"

Materials

- Coins that look similar (one for each child)
- Sticks of the same size that look similar (one for each child)

Benefits

Mindful Coins and Sticks improves focus, concentration, and attention. It also increases mindful awareness and visual recognition.

What to Say

- Mindfulness is paying attention to yourself and the world around you. When we practice mindfulness, it helps us focus. I'm going to hand you a coin. Carefully examine the coin. What do you see? Really notice all the details about your coin. We will try to find our coin in a bowl of other coins later, so we must pay close attention to all the details. How does your coin feel? Bring it up to your nose. What does your coin smell like? Great mindfulness!
- Place your coin in the basket. I'm going to mix up the coins.
- One by one I'm going to have you try to find your coin. You found it! Let's try it one more time, only this time let's use sticks.

CRAB SOCCER

Crab Soccer is a game where children pretend to be crabs in Crab Pose, but while being crabs they must keep a balloon in the air with their feet (sort of like juggling a soccer ball). Crab Pose may be a simple yoga pose, but when your child holds this pose and moves around the room, it becomes a challenging, strength-building activity.

Materials

- Balloon or beach ball

Benefits

Crab Soccer builds strength in the core, arms, and legs and also improves focus and coordination. This activity promotes teamwork and connectedness.

What to Say

- For this game, we are going to be crabs, but before we begin let's take a minute to check in with our breath. Sit up tall. Close your eyes. Take three deep breaths in and out through your nose. Notice your heartbeat and breath. Great.

- Let's get started! Sit on your bottom with your knees bent and feet flat on the floor. Put your hands on the floor behind you and have your fingers facing forward. Lift your belly up. You are a crab! Let's practice walking as a crab. Fantastic!

- Did you know crabs love to play soccer? I'm going to throw this balloon in the air. Imagine that it is a soccer ball. Try to keep the soccer ball from touching the ground by using your crab feet to kick it into the air. Great job! Notice your heartbeat and your breath.

- Let's relax now that we're done. How did this game include mindfulness?

Mindfulness Variation

Break groups of children into two teams with at least two team members on each team. Make a goal for each team out of pillows, bolsters, or yoga blocks. Have teams work together to make goals. The team with the most goals scored wins.

MINDFUL TIC-TAC-TOE

Mindful Tic-Tac-Toe offers a fresh and fun way to introduce mindfulness to your child using a classic children's game. Draw a tic-tac-toe grid (3 x 3 square grid). Next, write different mindfulness activities on a piece of paper. Cut the piece of paper into narrow slips and place the slips of paper in a container. You can choose from the list of mindfulness activities that follows or think of your own. After choosing and completing the mindfulness activity children can mark an "X" or "O" on the grid. Continue playing until one player has three marks in a row.

Here are a few mindfulness exercises to include:

- Notice your heartbeat and breath. Do ten jumping jacks. Notice your heartbeat and breath.
- Take ten Balloon Breaths (Chapter 3).
- Notice three sounds around you right now.
- Lie in Mummy Pose (Chapter 2) and take three Elevator Breaths (Chapter 3).
- Balance in Tree Pose (Chapter 2) for ten seconds on each foot with your eyes closed.
- Spin in a circle. Close your eyes. Name four green objects in the room.
- Lie on your back. Close your eyes. Scan your body and notice three sensations.
- Relax in Child's Pose (Chapter 2) for ten Hot Chocolate Breaths (Chapter 3).
- Take a deep breath in through the nose. What do you smell?

Here are some exercises that include props, if you have them available:

- Hula hoop for twenty seconds.
- Walk across the room with a beanbag on your head.
- Jump through a hopscotch game.
- Partners in Tree Pose hop across the room and back without falling.
- Jump rope for twenty seconds.

Materials

- Paper
- Pencil

Benefits

Mindful Tic-Tac-Toe increases mindful awareness in several ways. The breathing exercises enhance relaxation and feelings of well-being. Tic-Tac-Toe takes focus and concentration to win. Plus, this version of Tic-Tac-Toe provides a yoga pose, mindfulness, and breath work review.

What to Say

- Come to an Easy Seated Pose (Chapter 2). Place your hand in the bag and draw a slip of paper. We are going to do the activity on the piece of paper. Afterward you can place a mark on the tic-tac-toe grid.
- The player with three "Xs" or "Os" in a row is the winner!

MINDFUL JENGA

Test your mindful focus with this stacking game. Your child will need to be mindful when pulling out the right block and placing it on top or the whole tower will come tumbling down! Jenga is an entertaining game on its own, but adding mindfulness to it makes it even more engaging. Children love the giant Jenga, which is available online. On each wooden block, place a label with a mindfulness activity printed on it. After you or your child pull the block out, perform the mindfulness activity before placing the block on top of the tower.

Benefits

Mindful Jenga improves attention, focus, and concentration. The mindful exercises on the blocks increase mindful awareness and provide a sense of well-being. Taking turns improves social skills.

What to Say

- I've built a Mindful Jenga tower. We are going to take turns pulling out blocks, performing the activity on the block, and then placing the block on top of the tower. We have to be very mindful as we pull the blocks out and when we place them on top or the tower will fall over!
- Take a deep breath in. Let it all the way out. Good, now we are ready. Let's begin.

Mindfulness Variation

Up the focus by buying the multicolored Jenga set. Place different types of mindfulness activities on the various colors, such as putting labels with calming exercises on the blue blocks and labels with energizing activities on the red blocks. Make the game even more difficult by rolling the colored wooden die to determine which color of wooden block must be pulled.

RHYTHM DETECTIVE

Rhythm Detective is a group activity from Radiant Child Yoga, a children's yoga training program. Rhythm Detective requires mindful focus to detect who started a "movement chain." Children sit in Easy Seated Pose (Chapter 2) in a circle. One child is the detective. The detective briefly leaves the room. Another child starts the rhythm. The rhythm leader uses his hands or feet to have children clap, stomp, snap, or mimic whatever rhythm he chooses to create. The rhythm leader changes the rhythm randomly every few seconds. The detective returns and must figure out who the rhythm leader is. The detective is given only two guesses.

Benefits

Rhythm Detective enhances focus and creativity. It develops cooperation, teamwork, and connectedness. Rhythm Detective builds problem-solving and mindful awareness.

What to Say

- Let's make a big circle. Sit up tall in Easy Seated Pose (Chapter 2). Take three deep Balloon Breaths (Chapter 3). We are going to play Rhythm Detective! One person is going to be the rhythm leader and one person is going to be the detective. The detective will have two guesses to figure out who the rhythm leader is. The rhythm leader will lead the group in a series of rhythms.
- Let's practice with me being the leader. Just do what I do (clap hands, snap fingers, stomp feet). Great job!
- Who would like to volunteer to be the detective? Remember to use your mindfulness skills to figure out who the leader is. Our detective is going to leave the room briefly.
- Rhythm leader, give us a beat.
- Okay, detective, you can come back. Take your time, be mindful, and spot the leader.
- Great job figuring out who the leader was! Was it easy or difficult to figure out who the leader was? What mindfulness tools did you use as a detective?

SHAKE UP A ROUTINE

Shake Up a Routine is choosing an activity you do every day and doing it differently. When children perform the same routine daily or even weekly they go on autopilot and engage in the activity mindlessly. Shaking up routines can be as simple as moving your child's watch or Fitbit to the other wrist, having her walk on the other side of the street to school, or rearranging her bedroom. Changing up the routine helps children to be in the moment, which engages the brain and reduces stress.

Benefits

Shake Up a Routine enhances mindful awareness of the way things currently are. Changing things boosts creativity and teaches children that life is about more than routines. It also teaches adaptability, resiliency, and being able to "go with the flow" when things don't go as planned.

What to Say

- We are going to shake up our routine. Shaking up or changing things helps us be mindful and notice things we don't usually notice.
- Today we are going to do our yoga and mindfulness practice backward. We usually end with a meditation and "Namaste." Today we are going to start with taking a deep breath in as we sweep our arms out wide, then joining our palms together in Namaste Hands (Chapter 7) and saying "Namaste" as we bow forward. Next, we are going to listen to a relaxation story about Mindful Butterfly Meditation (Chapter 9).
- Next, we will practice mindfulness with Chime Listening (Chapter 4) and Mindful Eating (Chapter 5).
- Then, we will practice our yoga poses and play a high-energy game. Ready? Let's begin!

Mindfulness Variation

Other ways to shake up routines are to add spontaneous activities to the weekend, such as cooking breakfast foods for dinner, camping out in the living room, or eating dessert before dinner. There are endless ways to add new activities to your routine to mix it up for kids—and if you're out of ideas, your kids can suggest some!

CHAPTER 7

Mudras, Mind-Sets, and Positive Affirmations

Research shows us that consistently using hand movements, repeating positive statements, and changing perspective can help rewire the way children's brains and bodies behave, which can lead to healthy life habits. This chapter introduces you to mudras, mind-sets, and positive affirmations that can form new thought patterns, changing how your child feels.

Mudras

Mudras (pronounced "moo-drahs") are like yoga for your fingers. The patterns made by our fingers are believed to seal the energy in our body. Mudras come from India, but are practiced in many places all over the world. Mudras are usually practiced with yoga, breathing, relaxation, or meditation. Research shows us that mudras engage certain areas in the brain, creating a brain-body connection. Different areas of the hands are connected with different areas in the brain and body. When children place their hands in different mudras, it can activate a certain state of mind and thus can positively affect how the children feel. Mudras energize, focus, or calm the body, which make them a great tool for children, to help them regulate how they are feeling.

QUIET MUDRA

The Quiet Mudra is a gesture of quiet thought. In traditional meditation, this mudra brings to mind a bowl, which represents emptying the mind and focusing on the breath. This mudra helps children remember to watch their thoughts quietly and focus on their hands and breath.

Benefits

The Quiet Mudra enhances inner focus and calm. It is a good mudra for children to do before engaging in activities that involve focus or sustained concentration.

What to Say

- Sit up tall in Easy Seated Pose (Chapter 2). Begin to breathe in and out through your nose. We are going to do yoga with our fingers, which is called a mudra. Place the four fingers of both your hands in your lap like empty bowls. Place your left fingers on top of your right fingers. Touch your thumbs together. This is the Quiet Mudra.

- Let's take ten deep breaths as we practice this mudra. As you are breathing, notice the feeling between your thumbs. Can you feel the energy moving between your thumbs? Using your mindfulness skills, pay attention to all the sensations in your hands. What did you notice? How do you feel?

FOCUS MUDRA

The Focus Mudra is also known as Jnana Mudra and it is the most popular mudra in yoga. This fun and easy mudra is one that children recognize and will do with little instruction once they learn it. They automatically sit in Easy Seated Pose (Chapter 2), place their hands on their knees, touch their fingers together and say, "Ommm."

Benefits

The Focus Mudra helps children stay centered and focused on their breath. It is reported to enhance emotional and physical well-being. It clears the mind and promotes memory and concentration.

What to Say

- Sit up tall in Easy Seated Pose or stand up tall in Mountain Pose (Chapter 2) or even Tree Pose (Chapter 2). We are going to do yoga with our fingers, which is called a mudra. We are going to practice the Focus Mudra.
- Join the tip of your index finger with your thumb. Extend out your other fingers. Take a deep breath in. Let it out and say, "Ommm."

MIND-SET MUDRA

The Mind-Set Mudra is also referred to as the Ganesha Mudra in traditional yoga. Ganesha is a god who overcomes obstacles. Having a growth mind-set teaches children to persist with difficult tasks despite obstacles. Children go from saying, "I can't" to "I can't *yet*!"

Benefits

This mudra releases tension and tightness. Having a growth mind-set helps children realize that, with practice, they can accomplish anything. The Mind-Set Mudra encourages persistence, perspective, and practice.

What to Say

- We are going to do yoga with our fingers, which is called a mudra. Hold your left hand in front of your heart with your palm facing outward. Your fingers will point toward the right. Now grasp your left fingers with your right fingers, with the back of your hand facing outward (so your palms are facing each other). Take a deep breath in. As you breathe out, pull your hands apart while keeping your fingers gripped together. What do you feel? Are your arm muscles tight?
- As you continue to breathe, try to relax your arms. Take nine more breaths, tightening on the breath out, relaxing on the breath in. Release your hands. Notice what you feel.
- Shake it out. Let's switch our left and right hand positions and try it again.

COURAGE MUDRA

The Courage Mudra is also referred to as the Life or Pran Mudra. This simple mudra uses the pinky finger, ring finger, and thumb. There are a couple of variations in the placement of the two fingers. For example, Kim da Silva, a kinesiologist, suggests putting the thumb on the fingernails of the other two fingers instead of their tips to activate the right and left hemispheres of the brain. Or, you can do it as described in the exercise.

Benefits

The Courage Mudra relieves fatigue and nervousness. It also increases self-confidence and strength to try new things. When coupled with deep breathing, it has a calming and centering effect.

What to Say

- Sit or stand up tall in Easy Seated Pose (Chapter 2) or Mountain Pose (Chapter 2). We are going to do yoga with our fingers, which is called a mudra.
- With each hand, put the tips of your thumb, your little finger, and the finger next to your little finger (ring finger) together. Extend the other fingers out. This is the Courage Mudra. Close your eyes. Take ten deep Elevator Breaths (Chapter 3).

LOTUS MUDRA

The lotus is a beautiful flower that rises from its roots in the mud up through dark waters to bloom on the surface. The Lotus Mudra is traditionally placed at the heart to reflect love and kindness. Your child will place his hands in front of his heart and slowly open up his fingers like a lotus flower blossoming open. The purpose of the placement is for children to focus their attention on their heart, feeling it open with love for themselves and others.

Benefits

The Lotus Mudra combined with deep breathing releases stress and tension. It is a symbol for overcoming obstacles and persevering. The Lotus Mudra helps children focus and relax.

What to Say

- Did you know that the lotus flower grows in muddy water? We are going to make a lotus flower with our hands. We are going to do yoga with our fingers, which is called a mudra. Place both hands in front of your heart with your wrists, the bases of your palms, and only the edges of your hands and the pads of your pinky fingers and thumbs touching. This is the lotus bud.
- Let's make our lotus bloom. Imagine your lotus flower emerging from muddy waters and blossoming in the sunlight. Open your hands while maintaining contact between your palms, the edges of your hands and your pinkies, and your thumbs. Stretch the other fingers out wide. Take ten Elevator Breaths (Chapter 3).
- Now close your lotus flower back to a bud so it can sink under the water. Take ten Elevator Breaths. How do you feel?
- Let's talk about how the lotus flower represents the beauty and grace that is within all of us, but that has to overcome obstacles to bloom and show its beauty to the world.

Mindfulness Variation

The floating Lotus Mudra is an easy addition to this hand position. As you breathe in, slowly float your lotus flower toward your forehead. As you breathe out, slowly lower your lotus flower back to your heart. Continue this for ten breaths, imagining the lotus rising through the muddy waters to the sunlight.

BRAIN POWER MUDRA

The Brain Power Mudra is known as the Hakini Mudra. *Hakini* means "rule" or "power" in Sanskrit, the language of yoga. Many people unknowingly bring their fingers together in this manner while they are talking or thinking. The Brain Power Mudra incorporates breathing and a tongue position, and includes directing the eyes upward; therefore, the full version may be too difficult for young children due to the complexity. If so, they can practice the hand position and gradually add in the other elements.

Benefits

This mudra helps children focus and make decisions. It promotes a sense of calm and opens the mind to clearer thinking. Science reports the Brain Power Mudra can enhance memory and concentration.

What to Say

- Sit in Easy Seated Pose (Chapter 2). We are going to do yoga with our fingers, which is called a mudra.
- Raise your hands to your heart center and have your palms face each other. Bend your fingers a little and join the tips of your fingers on both hands together. This is the tricky part. Look up with only your eyes. Place your tongue on the roof of your mouth as you breathe in and let if fall down as you breathe out.

NAMASTE HANDS

Namaste is a greeting or gesture of thanks and peace. It demonstrates respect for others. Most yoga classes begin and end with Namaste Hands. Namaste Hands can also be incorporated into simple yoga poses, such as Tree, Airplane, or Mountain. This mudra is believed to calm thoughts, which can result in improved focus and concentration.

Benefits

Namaste Hands is calming and relaxing to children. Bringing the hands together at the heart harmonizes the right and left sides of the brain and may produce feelings of love, peace, and balance.

What to Say

- We are going to practice Namaste Hands! *Namaste* is a Sanskrit word that means, "I see what is special within you" or "I honor you."
- Bring your hands together at your heart center with palms touching. Close your eyes and begin to breathe in and out through your nose. Feel your belly rise as you breathe in and fall as you breathe out. Focus your attention on your hands. What do you notice?
- Now move your hands slowly up so that your thumbs are touching the area right between your eyebrows. This is referred to as your "third eye" in yoga, but it is also where our thinking brain is located. The thinking brain helps us make good decisions. Close your eyes and focus on your hands. What did you notice? Was it different from when your hands were at your heart?

SINGING MUDRA

Singing Mudra is referred to as Sa Ta Na Ma meditation or Kirtan Kriya in Kundalini yoga. It is a powerful meditation that science has shown to have benefits to the brain, such as improving memory (most research is in connection to Alzheimer's disease); reducing stress hormones and inflammation; enhancing cerebral blood flow; increasing feel-good brain chemicals (dopamine and serotonin); and improving sleep, mood, and cognition. This mudra requires the fingers to move instead of being held still. Educators and therapists use this mudra to help children with learning problems because of its positive effects on brain health, such as improved memory and cognition.

Benefits

This mudra promotes brain activity and relaxes the nerves. Certain sounds carry a vibration that can provide children with energy and help them focus. *Sa, Ta, Na,* and *Ma* are some of those sounds. They give your child focus and add a special energy to the meditation. Science shows us that this mudra can improve short-term memory and improve your child's mood.

What to Say

- We are going to do yoga with our fingers, which is called a mudra. After we practice the yoga with our fingers, we are going to add some sounds to it.
- First, press your thumb and your first finger together. Next, press your thumb and middle finger together. Now, press your thumb and ring finger together. Finally, press your thumb and little finger together. Let's practice one more time before we add sound. Ready? Go. Great mudras!
- Let's add the sounds to help us focus. While slowing saying "SA," press your thumb to the pad of your first finger. On "TA" press your thumb and middle finger together. On "NA" press your thumb and ring finger together. And on "MA" press your thumb and little finger together.
- Say "SATANAMA" out loud over and over again for one minute, then whisper it for the same amount of time. Next, hear it inside your mind while you silently keep moving your fingers for two minutes, and whisper it again for one minute. Finally, say it out loud for one more minute. This should add up to six minutes.

Positive Affirmations

Research has shown us that children are more likely to focus on negative thoughts than positive ones. Yet negative attitudes increase stress chemicals in the brain and can result in a negative attitude about ourselves and the world. Teaching children to accept negative emotions and to neither avoid nor dwell on them helps them to deal with difficult emotions in a healthy way.

Positive affirmations help children to think positively and believe in themselves. They are repeated phrases that focus on what your child wants out of life. Emphasizing positive thinking and positive affirmations allows children to build new skills, such as resiliency, confidence, and positivity. Modeling and sharing positivity with your child are powerful ways to teach it. Positivity is like any skill: children must practice positivity to be more positive.

Here are some tips for developing positive affirmations for children:

- **Keep them short and formed in the present tense.** For example, "I am calm" is a powerful affirmation.
- **Encourage repetition.** Have your child repeat the affirmation over and over again.
- **Make them meaningful.** The affirmation should be something that resonates with your child and use words they understand.
- **Use only positive statements.** Instead of saying, "I will no longer be unhappy," which is confirming a negative statement, say, "I am happy!"

PEACEMAKERS

PeaceMakers is a game that can be purchased online from *Generation Mindful* (www.genmindful.com). PeaceMakers teaches children to share their feelings in fun ways. PeaceMakers cards are full of positive affirmations to enhance social and emotional skills in children.

Materials

- PeaceMakers game

Benefits

PeaceMakers builds confidence, self-esteem, and positivity, and reinforces a growth mind-set.

What to Say

- Let's sit in a circle. We are going to play a mindfulness game called PeaceMakers.
- Why do you think the card game is called PeaceMakers? Yes, because it is a game to help you feel more peaceful. Are you ready? Let's begin!
- PeaceMakers can be played several different ways. Today we are going to pick a card and write or draw our card as it relates to our life. If you can't think of what to draw or write, I will help you.

AFFIRMATION CARDS

Affirmation Cards is a fun art activity. Positive affirmations are more successful if your child develops his or her own positive words. The power of positive self-talk isn't in saying the words, but in believing them. Your child must internalize the positive statements.

Materials

- Lifestyle or mindfulness magazines
- Patterned scrapbook paper
- Scissors
- Glue
- Clear packing tape
- Ring holder
- Hole puncher
- Colored index cards
- Colored pencils
- Stickers

Benefits

Allowing your child to create her own affirmations gives her ownership and commitment to the positive words. Making positive statements engages your child and helps enhance positivity.

What to Say

- Affirmations are positive words we say to ourselves. Let's use these index cards to make our own positive affirmations.
- First, let's decorate our cards. Place stickers or draw hearts, swirls, dots, or any shapes you like on your cards. Look through magazines to find words or phrases that inspire you. Write "I am" and then paste the word you have found after it. To protect our cards we are going to stick this clear packing tape

around them. Great! Now punch a hole in the top corner and let's place them on the ring holder. Here are a few affirmation ideas:

  - I am peaceful.
  - I can do whatever I focus my mind on.
  - I am happy.
  - I love learning new things.
  - I am magnificent.
  - I am flexible.
  - I am healthy.
  - I am confident.
  - I am full of energy.
  - I am strong.

- Now that we have made our Affirmation Cards, let's talk about how we can use them. You could start your day off on a positive note by reading through your cards first thing in the morning and then revisit them again before going to bed at night. If you are having a rough day, grab your affirmation cards and read through them. Can you think of any other times you'd want to use your cards?

HAPPY BOX

Accomplishment takes hard work, and your child should recognize that. The Happy Box is a treasure box of things your child has accomplished that makes him feel good. It could be a note from a teacher or friend, sports medal, pictures of success, or a ribbon from the fair. It is a box filled with accomplishments and things that make your child feel happy and positive. Some days it's hard to feel positive and happy, but instead of focusing on what is wrong, the Happy Box helps children focus on what is right so they can change their negative outlook to a positive one.

Materials

- Small box
- Positive words
- Scrapbook paper

Benefits

The Happy Box promotes positive self-talk, creativity, overall well-being, and feelings of calmness. It helps build self-esteem and improves behavior, attitude, and achievement.

What to Say

- You are going to make your box into your very own Happy Box. Feel free to decorate it in any way that makes you feel happy.
- Next, we will fill it with all the fantastic things you have accomplished. Whenever you are feeling grumpy or sad, you can take out your Happy Box and look at all the things you have accomplished. Let's start filling up your box!

AMAZING JOURNAL

There are beautiful and amazing details everywhere around us, but sometimes we miss these simple pleasures. The Amazing Journal helps children notice simple and amazing things that are present every day. Your child will journal all the amazing things she notices in life. It could be a rainbow, spider web, or maybe the ocean. She will take a picture, draw, or just write down what she finds amazing. At the end of the week, discuss and reflect with your child on all the amazing things she has seen and recorded in her journal.

Benefits

Amazing Journal helps children slow down and notice the simple beauty in the world around them. It enhances mindful awareness, reflection, and connectedness.

What to Say

- Start by making a cover for your journal with the word "Amazing" in the center. Define what *amazing* means to you.
- As you go about your day, notice things that are amazing to you. Take a picture, draw a picture, or just write it down. Place it in your Amazing Journal.
- At the end of the week we will look at the items together. I can't wait to see what you put in your journal!

AFFIRMATION WEB

The Affirmation Web requires a group of slightly older children. Children will sit in a circle and generate affirmations about themselves while hanging onto the strand of yarn coming out of a ball. Then they will roll the ball to another child while still holding the strand. The next child will state an affirmation about himself, such as "I am flexible" while grasping the dangling strand, then will roll the ball to another child. This continues until each child has stated an affirmation and a web is formed. Afterward a piece of the yarn will be cut off to make a bracelet for each child.

Materials

- Ball of yarn
- Scissors

Benefits

Positive affirmations help children reach goals they have set for themselves. The Affirmation Web develops connectedness alongside social and cooperation skills. This game also gives children a tangible reminder of their affirmation, which will keep them focused and on-task to completing their affirmation goal.

What to Say

- Let's begin by sitting in a circle. We are going to make an Affirmation Web! Affirmations are short, positive phrases that focus on what you want out of life. For example, if you have too much homework, basketball practice after school, and your sister has a play you need to attend, then you may be feeling overwhelmed with life and your affirmation could be "I am calm and peaceful."
- Sit up tall in Easy Seated Pose (Chapter 2). Let's close our eyes and take three slow Balloon Breaths (Chapter 3). Great breathing!
- With your eyes closed, think of an affirmation about yourself. Remember, it should be positive and short. I'll start by saying my affirmation and then, while I hang onto this string of yarn, I'm going to roll the ball of yarn to the next person, and they will say their affirmation. We will continue until everyone has stated an affirmation and is holding onto the yarn.
- Wow! What a wonderful Affirmation Web we have built. I'm going to come around and cut off the piece of the web you are holding. We will tie shorter pieces of the yarn around our wrists as reminders of our affirmation.

AFFIRMATION ART

Affirmation Art allows children to see their affirmation goals and be creative. Drawing affirmations is a perfect mindful activity for children to de-stress and relax.

Materials

- Poster board
- Colored pencils
- Ambient music

Benefits

Pictures and words can help make goals and affirmations more concrete for children and thus easier to work toward. Developing and hanging a poster board is a great visual reminder and motivator for children.

What to Say

- I'm going to play some relaxing music. Sit up tall in Easy Seated Pose. Close your eyes and take ten deep breaths in and out through your nose.
- While you are breathing, think of an affirmation about yourself. It can be a goal you want to accomplish or just a positive statement that makes you feel good. Okay, now open your eyes. Great breath work!
- Did everyone come up with an affirmation? We are going to draw a picture of our affirmation on this poster board. Here is an example. I am scared of heights, so my affirmation is about being brave and facing my fears. I wrote, *I am brave*, in the middle of my poster board. Then I drew myself on the top of a mountain, walking across a high rope bridge, and climbing to the top of a treehouse.

PASS THE AFFIRMATION

Pass the Affirmation is a group activity for children ages eight and up. Children write their names on a piece of paper and then pass the paper around the circle so everyone in the group has a chance to write something positive about each person in the group.

Benefits

Pass the Affirmation encourages a change in perspective. It empowers children, creates connectedness, and dissipates negativity.

What to Say

- Let's sit in a circle. I'm going to give each of you a piece of paper. I want you to write your name at the top. Now pass the paper to the person sitting on your right. Write one positive or nice thing about the person whose name is at the top of the piece of paper. Each person writes one positive statement. Remember to keep your comments positive and kind.
- When you've written your positive statement, pass the piece of paper to the person sitting to your right until it gets back to the original person.
- Once your paper is returned to you, read the kind statements about yourself. Take in a deep breath. Let it out. Notice how you feel.

VISION BOARD

A vision board is a visual representation of things your child wants to accomplish. For this activity, you'll play ambient music and allow your child to be creative and mindful while creating his board. Begin by asking your child to come up with three goals he would like to accomplish and then ask how he will accomplish them. After he has determined his goals, find some pictures or words that represent the skills and positive qualities that will assist him in reaching his goals. Cut them out and paste them on the Vision Board. Hang the Vision Board in the child's room.

Materials

- Ambient music
- Poster board
- Magazines
- Scissors
- Colored pencils
- Glue stick
- Poster board letters or stencil

Benefits

Vision Board helps children visualize their goals. When children achieve a goal, it boosts their self-confidence. Accomplishing goals also teaches children to have a growth mind-set and believe in their ability to accomplish more challenging goals.

What to Say

- Who likes to make art projects? Me too! We are going to make Vision Boards. A Vision Board is a poster that has pictures and words that represent goals we would like to accomplish. Accomplishing goals takes hard work and persistence, and our Vision Board will remind us to keep trying!
- Let's start by brainstorming three goals we would like to accomplish in the next year. These could be learning to play the guitar, being able to do a handstand, or even being more mindful.
- Once you've figured out your goals, start to look for pictures and words that relate to your goal. For example, if doing a handstand is your goal, look for words such as *strength*, *upside down*, *yoga*, and *practice*. Cut out the words or pictures and post them to your board.
- When we are finished, we will hang our Vision Boards in a spot where we can see them every day to remind us to keep practicing.

Mindful Mind-Set

Dr. Carol Dweck, professor of psychology at Stanford University, describes a *growth mind-set* as a belief system that intelligence and ability can be developed. This mind-set asserts that with effort and persistence, people can grow their cognitive ability. Teaching children about the growth mind-set helps them learn about the plasticity of the brain, meaning that they can actually change their brains through practice and resiliency. Dweck defines the term *fixed mind-set* to describe people who believe that cognitive ability is something that they are born with and that doesn't change. A child with a fixed mind-set may be afraid to try new things or believe that she will never be good at difficult tasks. This is why it is important to emphasize effort instead of innate ability when praising children. Praising effort results in a growth mind-set! This is what the following exercises will help cultivate.

MIND-SET DANCE PARTY

This activity is for younger children, ages four to six years. *Sesame Street* has introduced some amazing growth mind-set songs, such as "Don't Give Up" by Bruno Mars and "The Power of Yet" by Janelle Monáe. The songs and videos are easily accessible on *YouTube*. Find and play your favorite while you and your child dance and sing the words. Afterward, talk about what message he or she learned from the song.

Benefits

Mind-Set Dance Party energizes and improves mood. It teaches children persistence and to not give up when things are challenging. The positive message in the song helps children change their mind-set and enhance their well-being.

What to Say

- Who wants to have a dance party? I am going to play some music about the power of *yet*, which means that if we keep trying even when things are hard, eventually we will be able to do the skill we are practicing.
- Let's place our hand on our hearts, close our eyes, and notice our breath and heartbeat.
- Okay, now open your eyes. When I play the music, dance and sing along with the words. Now that the music has stopped, let's find our breath and heartbeat again. Have they changed? Yes, they are faster.
- What were some things that were hard for the characters in the song? Can you think of something that is difficult right now that you want to be better at? Great examples. How can you get better at it? Right, you keep trying.

FANTASTIC ELASTIC BRAIN

Growth mind-set comes from understanding that the brain can change, grow, and learn new things with practice. *Your Fantastic Elastic Brain* is a children's book by JoAnn Deak that teaches children that they have the ability to stretch and grow their brains. After reading the story, bring out the stretchy band and do movement activities that demonstrate how the brain grows with exercise, new challenges, and even with making mistakes.

Materials

- Bear Paw Creek Medium Stretchy Band (holds sixteen children)
- *Your Fantastic Elastic Brain* by JoAnn Deak

Benefits

The Fantastic Elastic Brain develops cooperation, growth mind-set, and teamwork. It enhances focus and mindful awareness.

What to Say

- Let's sit in a circle. We are going to read a book called *Your Fantastic Elastic Brain*.
- Now that we've read the book, we are going to play an elastic brain game with a giant stretchy band. Let's stand up inside the stretchy band. Can someone explain what a fixed mind-set is? Great explanation! I'm going to say a fixed mind-set statement. When I call on you, I want you to change it to a growth mind-set statement. Fixed statements don't stretch your brain, so if you can't think of a statement, we will just stay still. If the statement you suggest isn't a growth mind-set statement, we will take a step in. Growth statements grow and stretch your brain, so we will take one step backward, making the stretchy band bigger. Here are some examples of how to change a fixed mind-set statement into a growth mind-set one.

Instead of saying:	Try saying:
I'm not good at this.	I can learn anything I want to with a good attitude and enough effort!
It is good enough.	I can do better!
I give up.	I'll keep trying until I get it.
This is too hard.	This may take some time, but I'll keep trying.
I made a mistake.	Mistakes help me to learn and stretch my brain.
She is so smart, I will never be that smart.	I'm going to figure out how she does it and train my brain to be just as smart.
I can't do this.	I can't do this yet.
I don't like to be challenged.	I love to challenge myself.

BUBBLE GUM BRAIN

Read aloud the book *Bubble Gum Brain* by Julia Cook. *Bubble Gum Brain* endorses the power of "yet" and teaches children that is okay to make mistakes, because that is how we stretch and grow our brains. After reading the book, reflect and review with your child by drawing a fixed mind-set brain (brick) and a growth mind-set brain (bubble gum) and then allow children to draw their own mind-set brain. Ask them to write thought bubbles around each brain to describe the different mind-sets.

Materials

- *Bubble Gum Brain* by Julia Cook
- Colored pencils
- Paper
- Ambient music

Benefits

Bubble Gum Brain offers an opportunity for children to explore mind-sets and identify and label a fixed mind-set and growth mind-set. This activity allows children to be creative with their mind-set and expand upon what they have learned.

What to Say

- We are going to read a book called *Bubble Gum Brain*.
- Now that we have read the story, we are going to draw a fixed mind-set brain, a growth mind-set brain, and we are going to create our own mind-set brain. That's right, make your own mind-set brain with whatever substance you want. Be sure to name it! Let's take three Elevator Breaths (Chapter 3). Ready. Set. Draw.

WHAT AM I?

One way to communicate the idea of perspective to children is to have them close their eyes, then pass around a small wooden toy and have each child feel the toy for five seconds. Once each child has had a chance to feel the object, have them write down or draw what toy they were holding. Then allow children to talk among themselves and collaborate to determine what the wooden toy is.

Materials

- Paper bag
- Wooden toy

Benefits

This activity teaches children that others have perspectives or views that are different from their own regarding the same event. Children begin to realize that even though others have different ideas, it doesn't make them wrong. This activity teaches your child to not make quick judgments, which is an important aspect of mindfulness.

What to Say

- Let's sit in a circle. I'm going to pass around an object in a bag. Your job is to reach in with your hand and feel it for five seconds. You can't peek or look at the object. You must engage your mindfulness skills to determine what is in the bag. To make sure we don't peek, we are all going to close our eyes and turn our head to the side. Keep your guess to yourself.
- Now that everyone has had a chance to feel the object, we are going to draw or write down what we think it is.
- Now that everyone has drawn the object, I want you to discuss it as a group and come up with an answer based on your conversation. Remember, you had only a few seconds to feel the object, so someone else may have felt a different part of the object. That means everyone may have a different answer. To figure out the mystery of the object, you must all work together. Remember to be mindful and avoid labeling guesses as "good" or "bad."

PERSPECTIVE ART

This activity requires a 3-D puzzle, such as a Rubik's Cube or Pyramid, both of which can be purchased inexpensively online. Place the 3-D puzzle in front of a group of children. Ask each child to draw the 3-D puzzle from where they are sitting. Then have children compare their drawings and perspectives.

Materials

- Paper
- Crayons
- 3-D puzzle (Rubik's Cube or Pyramid)

Benefits

Perspective drawing focuses attention while soothing the central nervous system. It builds mindful awareness and perspective taking in a noncompetitive manner.

What to Say

- Let's make a circle around the puzzle. I'm going to give you a piece of paper and some crayons. I want you to draw the puzzle exactly as you see it. Mindfully observe the object from where you are sitting and then draw just what you see.
- These are wonderful drawings. Now find a partner and compare your drawings. You both drew the same object; do they look the same or different? How are they the same? How are they different? Is it okay to have different views or perspectives?

CHAPTER 8

Kindness and Gratitude

We hear all the time about how small acts of kindness have a powerful impact on others. Science demonstrates that performing an act of kindness, even if it's as simple as holding a door open for a stranger, can boost happiness for both parties. This means kindness is contagious—when your child does a kind act for someone, it leads to that person also doing a kind act for someone else.

Not only can a random act of kindness lift your child's mood, it can also reduce stress and build the immune system, resulting in a healthier child. Being kind to others, the environment, and himself helps your child develop the social and emotional skills he needs to be resilient and happy. Being kind to others has been found to increase energy levels and confidence. Thus, the good vibes your child receives from others when they complete a kind act translates to helpful benefits for themselves. When a child becomes more aware of his own kind behavior, it improves his overall well-being. But kindness, like any other skill, takes practice. Kindness can be taught in the home, classroom, or even during a yoga class. Kindness can be simple and only take a few minutes, but it is important to build it into your child's day.

Hand-in-hand with kindness comes gratitude. When children practice being grateful, it helps them develop a better understanding of other people's feelings. In this chapter, you will find activities to foster gratitude and kindness. Family games and art projects are included to extend the connecting activities to the entire family. These activities serve as a way to initiate a practice of gratitude and kindness to assist your child and/or family any time there is a need for a new perspective, mood transformation, or improved health.

Gratitude

Encouraging children to think of things they are grateful for or that they appreciate activates the calming part of the nervous system. This helps children feel calmer and happier. Science tells us that being grateful increases levels of the feel-good chemicals in the brain, which, in turn, results in children having higher achievement in school, a more positive attitude, and improved focus.

GRATITUDE JOURNAL

This activity involves either creating a Gratitude Journal or printing one out for free from an online source. To make the Gratitude Journal a healthy habit, have your child write or draw in his journal at the same time every day. Some parents like to have their children start their day with an "Attitude of Gratitude." Every morning before school, have your child write or draw one thing he is grateful for in his journal. When children appreciate the goodness in their lives, they feel compelled to give back to others. What a great way for your child to start his day! Here are a few ideas to get your child started. Ask him to write or draw about:

- A person you appreciate.
- A place that makes you feel happy.
- An item you love (e.g., backpack, waffles, school).
- A skill or ability you are awesome at.
- A person that makes you laugh.
- Your favorite song.
- Something that you accomplished that made you feel good.
- A sport or hobby you enjoy.
- A pet you love.
- A teacher or coach who showed you kindness.

Materials

- Notebook or journal
- Pen

Benefits

Learning to be grateful helps children to develop executive functioning skills, mindful awareness, and compassion for others. Being grateful can shift your child's mood and enhance her overall well-being.

What to Say

- Did you know that practicing being grateful can make you feel happier and healthier? We are going to make this notebook into a Gratitude Journal. Let's draw a couple of things that you are grateful for on the front of it.
- Each morning, think of one thing you are grateful for and write or draw it in your Gratitude Journal. If you are feeling grumpy, stressed, or sad, read through your Gratitude Journal and remember all the good things you have to be thankful for in your life.

GRATITUDE ROCK

A Gratitude Rock is a symbol or visual reminder of gratitude. This activity is simple, but can have a powerful effect on your child's mood. While enjoying a mindful walk with your child, ask her to find a small rock. When you return home, have her write or draw something on it that she is grateful for. If your child is having a bad day or feeling sad, have her hold the rock and take ten deep breaths. As she breathes, have her look at the Gratitude Rock to shift her perspective and produce a sense of inner peace.

Materials

- Rock
- Markers

Benefits

The Gratitude Rock promotes appreciation and mindful reflection. It can help your child be happier and calmer. The Gratitude Rock serves as an anchor or a symbol to focus attention and balance energy.

What to Say

- Let's go for a Mindful Walk (Chapter 2). While we are walking, let's look for a special rock to make our Gratitude Rock. Perfect.
- Now that we're back, let's wash off our rock and write or draw on it something that you are grateful for. Feel free to decorate it anyway you like. Maybe add a heart with a special name in the middle of it, the sun, or your pet. This is your special Gratitude Rock.
- Now that your rock has what you are grateful for on it, cup it with both hands and hold it in front of your heart. Look at your Gratitude Rock as we take three deep Elevator Breaths (Chapter 3). Concentrate on the image or word you have drawn on your rock.
- Set your rock down. Notice how you feel. Place your Gratitude Rock in your pocket or backpack and bring it out when you are feeling sad or stressed. You can also take it out throughout the day as a reminder of the things you are grateful for. This can be done several times a day, to give yourself a mini mindfulness moment whenever and wherever you need it. During these moments, take three Elevator Breaths, as we just did, and notice if it changes how you feel.

GRATITUDE ALPHABET

Help your child develop gratitude by listing something he is grateful for using each letter of the alphabet. When children pay attention to the good things around them, it helps them notice and appreciate all the good things they have in their lives. Sometimes it is hard to think of things for every letter, so allow your child to skip around and be creative when dealing with the harder letters, such as "Z." Also, encourage your child to write down his list so that he can refer back to it when he needs to see the positive aspects of life.

Materials

- Paper
- Colored pencils

Benefits

Having children develop a list of things they are grateful for can shift their mood. Gratitude Alphabet builds mindful awareness, optimism, and gratitude. Gratitude can rewire the brain to appreciate the things in life that are going well.

What to Say

- I have a sheet of paper with each letter of the alphabet on it. For each letter of the alphabet, I want you to write down a word that describes something you are grateful for. For example, for the letter "A" I wrote "apples," because I love to eat apples as a healthy snack. What would you like to write for "A"?
- If you can't think of anything for a letter, skip it and then come back to it at a later time and we can brainstorm together.

Mindfulness Variation

For younger children, make Gratitude Alphabet into a game. Have your child pick a letter out of a pile and ask him to come up with one thing he's thankful for that starts with that letter.

VOLUNTEER WORK

Giving back to the community, in even small ways, can foster a sense of belonging, positivity, and gratitude. Helping others can be as simple as assisting a younger sibling with homework or cleaning up, giving clothes that no longer fit to Goodwill, or bringing canned goods to a shelter or family in need. Volunteer Work consists of helping your child find her volunteer niche, something that resonates with her. Children learn and imitate behaviors they see others performing, which is called observational learning. Modeling Volunteer Work and accompanying your child to help others will have a powerful impact and teach your child valuable life skills.

Benefits

Volunteering helps children connect to others. Volunteer Work promotes empathy, compassion, and kindness. This activity can lead to more open-mindedness and improved overall well-being.

What to Say

- Each week, we are going to engage in Volunteer Work. We will spend some time helping people or animals around us. These can even be people who live in our own house!
- Let's write down a list of ways we can help others, especially those who may not have as much as we do. Then we will pick one and do our best to engage in Volunteer Work at least one time a week.

I AM AWESOME

I Am Awesome involves having your child write down ten things she is awesome at. Your child will think of all the awesome things her friends and family have told her she is good at and all the things she believes she is awesome at doing, such as drawing, singing, or playing an instrument. Having your child make a list of all her good traits will help her to remember all the great gifts she has in her life.

Materials

- Colored pencils
- Paper
- Ambient music

Benefits

Being grateful can be uplifting, and in addition, it increases mindful awareness and self-awareness. Breathing deeply helps children to relax and de-stress.

What to Say

- Let's make a list of all the things we are awesome at. This is not bragging or being boastful. It is just a list that reminds us to be grateful for all of the things we are good at. It can be praise that you have heard from your friends or family. The comments can be small or big.
- Listen to the peaceful music, smile, and breathe in and out as you draw and/or write your list.
- Now that you have made your list, sit up tall in Easy Seated Pose (Chapter 2) and close your eyes. Begin to use Elevator Breaths (Chapter 3), feeling your belly rise as you breathe in, and fall as you breathe out. Start to think about your list and all the wonderful things you are awesome at. As you breathe out, whisper "I Am Awesome!" After ten breaths, thank yourself one last time for being awesome.

SETTLED GLITTER DRAWING

This activity teaches children how gratitude can help them feel better when they are feeling upset, that is, when their "glitter"—their thoughts, feelings, and behaviors—have become unsettled. Children will draw a picture of themselves when they are feeling stressed. After discussing five things they are grateful for, and taking a few deep breaths, children will draw another picture showing themselves feeling settled and calm. Discuss the pictures with the children. You may ask, "What are some of the differences between your two pictures? What are some tools you can use to settle your glitter? How does thinking of things that you appreciate make you feel?"

Materials

- Paper
- Colored pencils

Benefits

This activity helps children deepen their awareness of their own mental processes, which leads to more mindful awareness and reflection. It strengthens decision-making and builds resiliency.

What to Say

- Let's draw a picture today of what our bodies look like when we are worried or feeling stressed about something that is happening in our lives. Think of an event that has unsettled your glitter recently—remember, your glitter is your thoughts, feelings, and behaviors. Draw a picture of yourself when your glitter was unsettled. As you draw, remember to keep breathing in and out through your nose. What do your face and hair look like? What about your hands? Let's make some thought bubbles to show what is going on in your brain, or even write a few words to describe the feeling.
- Did you know practicing gratitude can make you feel calmer and happier? What are five things you are grateful for? Those are wonderful things to be grateful for! Take five deep Balloon Breaths (Chapter 3).
- Now let's write down the five things we are thankful for and draw a picture of ourselves when our glitter is settled and we are feeling calm and happy. Let's compare and talk about our drawings.

FAMILY GRATITUDE BOOK

A Family Gratitude Book is a book that each family member contributes to and builds weekly to instill an "attitude of gratitude" in family members. Anyone in your family can write or include what they feel grateful for, in the form of photos, drawings, poems, notes, and/or other items. Place the book somewhere that is visible, like a coffee table in the living room, and encourage family members to contribute weekly. At the end of the week, have a family meeting and discuss all the new items that have been added that week.

Materials

- Scrapbook
- Scrapbook paper
- Markers, colored pencils, or crayons

Benefits

A Family Gratitude Book encourages connection and promotes positive communication. It teaches gratitude and mindful reflection. The Family Gratitude Book enhances creativity and fine motor skills.

What to Say

- I've bought a scrapbook, which is going to become our Family Gratitude Book. Let's decorate the front cover. Should we place this picture of our family on the front? What else can we add? Our names? A title?
- Once a week, each family member is going to add something for which they're grateful. At the end of the week, we will have a show-and-tell to talk about and show each other what amazing things we have added for the week.
- What is something you could add this week? It can be anything you are grateful to have in your life. For example, I'm adding a picture of my bike to the Family Gratitude Book. Yesterday the weather was nice and I was able to ride my bike on a beautiful trail. I was very grateful for the weather and my bike. What are you grateful for this week? Let's add it to the book!

GRATITUDE WALK

A Gratitude Walk is going for a stroll in nature with your child and looking around at all the things in nature you are grateful for. There is so much for children to appreciate in nature, such as the streams, the smell of rain, and the sound of birds chirping. Walk slowly and mindfully, noticing sights, sounds, smells, and even textures to engage all the senses, making it a Gratitude Walk that your child will remember.

Benefits

Gratitude Walk promotes mindful awareness, appreciation for nature, and mindful reflection. It enhances attention, concentration, and focus.

What to Say

- Let's go for a Gratitude Walk! Before we begin walking, let's take three deep Balloon Breaths (Chapter 3) together. Remember to walk slowly, noticing every step you take. This is a mindful Gratitude Walk, so we want to use all of our senses.
- Look all around you. What are some things that you are grateful for that you see? Trees are a wonderful thing to be grateful for. Let's place our hands on the tree and notice what it feels like. It is hard and the bark is rough. What does the tree look like? Very tall, brown, and green. Yes, great description! Take a deep breath in through your nose. What do you smell?
- Let's continue walking and see what other wonderful things await us.

GRATITUDE STICKS

This is a twist on the classic game Pick-Up Sticks. The Pick-Up Sticks game can be purchased online and includes blue, red, green, yellow, and black sticks. For each color, assign a different gratitude theme. Drop the sticks so that they scatter on top of one another. The object of the game is to pick up a stick without moving the other sticks. Once your child successfully picks up a stick, she then answers the gratitude question connected to that particular color. The child with the most sticks wins. After the activity, ask your child or the group about how this game is connected to mindfulness.

Here are some examples of gratitude themes to include:

- **Blue stick:** Name a friend you appreciate.
- **Red stick:** Name a food you are grateful for and the person who made it possible for you to eat it.
- **Green stick:** Name a family member you are grateful for and tell us why you chose this person.
- **Yellow stick:** Name something in nature you appreciate.
- **Black stick:** Name an animal you are grateful for and tell us why you chose this animal.

Materials

- Pick-Up Sticks game

Benefits

Gratitude Sticks builds teamwork and connectedness. It promotes focus, appreciation, and concentration. Plus, it's a game that encourages stress-free, fun competition.

What to Say

- We are going to play a game called Gratitude Sticks. Gratitude Sticks is similar to a game called Pick-Up Sticks, but I've added a gratitude twist. On the dry erase board, I've color-coded the different sticks so that they are linked with a gratitude activity. For example, if a blue stick is picked up without moving any other stick, you will name a friend you appreciate and then you get to keep that stick. The person with the most sticks at the end of the game wins. Ready? Let's play!

- Fantastic job focusing and picking up sticks. Can you tell me how this game is mindful? Exactly, you have to pay attention with all of your senses or else you will move another stick.

GRATITUDE TREE

Gratitude Tree is a group activity that can be completed in a family or class setting. This art activity uses tree branches or twigs, construction paper, a leaf template, hole puncher, string, vase, and something for the bottom of the vase to hold the branches in place, such as stones or marbles. Place the stones or marbles at the bottom of a vase, then add the twigs. Next, trace the leaf template and cut out the leaf shape to make a pile of leaves. Punch a hole in the leaves and loop a piece of string through it (help the younger children if necessary). Have members of your family or class write or draw something they are grateful for once a day on a leaf and hang it on a branch. For some extra sparkle, add a string of white LED lights.

Materials

- Large twigs or small branches from local art store
- Construction paper
- Leaf template
- Hole puncher
- String
- Vase
- Marbles or stones for bottom of vase

Benefits

The Gratitude Tree helps instill a gratitude practice into children's daily lives. Creating leaves involves tracing, cutting, and hole punching, which enhances fine motor skills. The Gratitude Tree promotes a sense of connectedness, encourages reflection, and lifts mood.

What to Say

- Let's make a Gratitude Tree! A Gratitude Tree is a tree we create that has leaves with grateful messages written on them. Appreciating things, people, or places can help us feel happier and more mindful.
- Let's start by making the tree. We are going to put marbles in this big glass vase. Great job!
- Next, let's plant some of these long twigs in the marbles. We have a tree!
- Now let's make it a Gratitude Tree. We need to make some leaves by tracing this pattern and cutting the leaves out. I love all the amazing colors of the leaves. Next, let's punch a hole in the top of each leaf, then we will thread a piece of string through it and tie it to make a circle.
- Every day, we will write or draw one thing that we are thankful for on a leaf and hang it on the tree. Let's make some gratitude leaves for our tree.

KINETIC SAND MESSAGES

Kinetic Sand Messages is a multisensory activity for children that requires a sensory table or shallow plastic container, kinetic sand, and a paper cut into strips with gratitude prompts written on them. Before beginning the activity, have the kids explore the kinetic sand mindfully by feeling, looking, smelling, and listening to it. Ideas for gratitude prompts for you to hide are listed here, or feel free to come up with your own prompts. You and your child can take turns finding the prompts and finishing the gratitude statement until all ten have been found. Afterward, allow your child to create something she was grateful for in the sand and try to guess what it is.

Gratitude prompts could include:

- I am grateful for two things I taste:
- I am grateful for two things I feel on the inside:
- I am grateful for two things I see:
- I am grateful for two things I hear:
- I am grateful for two things that are green:
- I am grateful for two things I touch or can feel:
- I am grateful for these two friends:
- I am grateful for these two adults:
- I am grateful for these two things that help me relax:
- I am grateful for these two activities:

Materials

- Kinetic sand
- Strips of paper with gratitude prompts
- Pen or colored pencils
- Sensory table or plastic container

Benefits

Kinetic Sand Messages encourages reflection and mindful awareness. The activity engages multiple senses, which helps the brain reinforce the gratitude lesson. This activity promotes creativity and a sense of calm.

What to Say

- We are going to explore this kinetic sand mindfully, find some gratitude messages that I've hidden in the sand, and then create something. Let's begin by being mindful. Then we can search in the sand for the messages that are hidden. Remember, being mindful means that we pay attention to something with all of our senses.
- Let's start by feeling the sand. What does it feel like? Now let's bring it up to our nose. What do you smell? Next, just play with the sand. What do you hear? We will skip tasting this one! Great mindfulness.
- Let's look for the gratitude messages that are hidden in the sand and respond to the messages. Fantastic job! You have so many things to be grateful for in your life. Go ahead and create one of the things we talked about while using the sand and I will try to guess what it is.

GRATITUDE HUNT

Gratitude Hunt is a fun adventure for young children that will get them moving. Your child will go on a hunt for the Gratitude Tree (in this chapter), but to find the tree he must make it across a river, jungle, and swamp. Each different region has different physical challenges. Once your child finds the Gratitude Tree, reads his leaf, and breathes, he can reflect on how he feels.

Benefits

The Gratitude Hunt infuses gratitude with physical movements. It is uplifting and teaches children self-regulation. It promotes yoga pose practice, mindful awareness, and reflection.

What to Say

- We are going on a hunt in search of the mysterious and amazing Gratitude Tree. This powerful tree can make us feel happier when we've had a bad day. Let's start our journey by army crawling through these hollow logs across the river. We have to be very quiet and careful, as we don't want the logs to roll into the river. Did everyone make it across the river?
- Next, we are going to jog through the jungle. The jungle can be a scary place with big animals, so we don't want to stay too long. Ready? Start to jog. Oh no! I see a cobra, but he won't bother us if he thinks we are a snake. Plant your feet, make a big balloon with your hands and pop it until it falls all the way to the ground. Come up into Cobra Pose (Chapter 2). Deep breath in. Let it out in a "hisss." One more time. We fooled him!
- Begin to jog again. I see a lion. We have to make him think we are lions too. Plant your feet, make a big balloon with your hands and pop it all the way to the ground. Do Lion's Pose with three big Lion's Breaths (Chapter 3). Fantastic, lions.
- Start to jog again. We are at the end of the jungle! I think I see the Gratitude Tree ahead, but it is still really far away. Let's ride our Yoga Bicycles (Chapter 2).
- Oh no, what is this...a mountain! Slowly climb up the giant mountain (Cross Crawls, Chapter 2). We made it to the tree!
- Pick up a leaf off the ground from underneath the Gratitude Tree. Let's form a circle and read our leaves. Take ten Balloon Breaths as you think about what is written on your leaf. Notice how you feel.

Kindness Activities

When a child becomes more aware of her own kind behavior, it improves her overall well-being. But kindness, like any other skill, takes practice. Kindness can be taught in the home, classroom, or even during a yoga class. Kindness can be simple and take only a few minutes, but it is important to build it into your child's day.

THE GREAT KINDNESS CHALLENGE

Happiness scientist Shawn Achor, author of *The Happiness Advantage*, found that if you do random acts of kindness for two minutes a day for twenty-one days, you can train your brain to be more positive. To help organize yourself, you can sign up for the Great Kindness Challenge, a program that increases kindness in schools, families, and organizations. Families can sign up for free online at the Great Kindness Challenge website (https://thegreatkindnesschallenge.com) and receive a free Kindness Checklist of fifty ways to be kind. Families are challenged to complete as many kind acts as possible.

Benefits

Science tells us that when you are kind, it leads to more positivity. As a bonus, when children are more positive, they are more creative and productive. The Great Kindness Challenge promotes connectedness, kindness, and empathy for others.

What to Say

- We are going to participate in the Great Kindness Challenge. Using this poster as our checklist, we are going to pick a kind act each week to complete. After we have completed the act of kindness, we are going to check it off our list.
- Since there are fifty activities it will take us fifty weeks to complete, which is just about a year! Remember that kindness is contagious, which means others can catch it easily, so when you are kind to someone, it reminds them to be kind to someone else, and it continues to spread. Let's sprinkle kindness like confetti! Which one should we do first?

DRAW LOVE

This activity lets you see what love looks like from your child's perspective. Ask your child to Draw Love from a mindfulness stance, incorporating all the senses: seeing, hearing, feeling, tasting, and smelling. Allow him to add glitter or an essential oil to incorporate as many senses in his picture as possible. Once it's finished, hang it on the wall to promote positive thinking.

Materials

- Colored pencils
- Card stock
- Art materials (glitter, foam hearts, glitter glue, fabric swatches)
- Essential oils
- Ambient music

Benefits

Draw Love promotes mindful reflection and awareness. This activity encourages creativity and kindness while developing fine motor skills. Engaging multiple senses activates multiple areas in the brain, which facilitates learning.

What to Say

- I've passed out a piece of paper, glitter, foam hearts, and crayons. We are going to draw a mindful picture of love. If a picture is mindful, what do you think that means? Yes, we are going to include all of our senses in our picture.
- This picture is love from your perspective. A perspective is a way of looking at something. Remember we all have different perspectives or mind-sets (Chapter 7), which means our drawings may differ, and that is okay. We won't judge any other drawings as "good" or "bad."
- If we were to draw love, what would it look like? What is its shape and color? Let's draw it. What does love sound like? Great ideas! How can we draw what it sounds like? What do you think it smells like? Would you like to add an oil or just draw the smell? What does love feel like? I have some different fabric swatches if you want to glue them to your picture so you are able to touch your picture too. Let's start drawing!

WALL OF LOVE

This simple kindness activity can be done anytime, but is especially fun during the month of February, when Valentine's Day occurs. Purchase heart-shaped sticky notes or make your own with red paper and tape. Each day, have your children write down something they love and post the note on a certain wall in your home. At the end of the month, your child will have a Wall of Love. Leave it up for a while or decorate a box and put all the heart sticky notes in it so your child can look back on them when she is feeling down or having a stressful day.

Materials

- Heart-shaped sticky notes
- Colored pencils

Benefits

Making a Wall of Love promotes positive thinking and infuses your house with joy and optimism. It's a great visual reminder of all the things your child has to be thankful for. A Wall of Love enhances mindful awareness and mindful reflection.

What to Say

- Today is the first day of the month. For each day of the month, we are going to write one thing we love on a red heart-shaped sticky note and put it on our wall. At the end of the month we will have a whole Wall of Love.

KINDNESS COINS

Kindness Coins are small plastic coins that can be purchased online. Kindness Coins encourage random acts of kindness. When you see your child engaging in an act of kindness, reward him with a Kindness Coin. Then encourage your child to give his Kindness Coin to someone whom he sees being kind. Kindness Coins are an easy way to reward children for acts of kindness. This builds a sense of community and results in children positively interacting with others.

Benefits

Kindness Coins remind children to look for and spread kindness. Kindness Coins help children build compassion and empathy. This activity reinforces positive behavior and good habits, which encourages more kind behavior.

What to Say

- I have a jar of Kindness Coins. When I see you being kind to yourself, your environment, or another person, I'm going to give you a Kindness Coin.
- Here's the catch: I don't want you to keep the coin; instead, I want you to notice someone being kind and give it to them. By giving it to someone else, you are spreading kindness. Ready? Let the kind acts begin!

HAVE YOU FILLED YOUR BUCKET TODAY?

This activity is based on a children's book by Carol McCloud, *Have You Filled a Bucket Today?* In the book, each person has an invisible bucket they carry with them. Kind acts fill the bucket and unkind acts empty the bucket. Kind or unkind actions can also fill or empty other people's buckets. The story teaches children that our actions affect not only how we feel, but how others feel as well. This activity involves reading the book, brainstorming ways to fill other people's buckets, and actually filling buckets when the kind acts are completed.

Materials

- Small buckets
- The book *Have You Filled a Bucket Today?* by Carol McCloud
- Sticky notes

Benefits

Stories are a pivotal way that young children can learn social and emotional skills. This story illustrates how kindness can fill buckets and make people feel good. Developing kindness shifts emotions and enhances mindful awareness.

What to Say

- Let's sit in a circle in Easy Seated Pose (Chapter 2). I'm going to read the book, *Have You Filled a Bucket Today?*
- Now that we have read the book, let's talk about it. What was the book about? What is a bucket dipper? Let's think of ways to fill empty buckets. Great ideas!
- Let's decorate and write our names on these empty buckets so each member of the family has their own bucket. The story tells us that when you fill someone's bucket it also fills your own bucket. That means that when a kind act is completed, both the person who completed the act (bucket filler) and the person whose bucket was filled will write the kind act on a sticky note and place it in the bucket.
- Once the buckets are full, we will review all the kind acts on the notes and have a bucket filler celebration!

Mindfulness Variation

For older children, read the book as a kindness meditation. Have them lie in a resting pose, such as Mummy Pose or Supported Fish (Chapter 2), on a small bolster or rolled-up mat. Place an eye pillow over their eyes and play soft ambient music. Read the story as a loving-kindness meditation. Afterward, discuss the book with them.

PAY IT FORWARD

Pay It Forward is completing a random act of kindness to a teacher, friend, or family member. Pay It Forward acts may include: holding a door open for someone, letting someone go in front of you in line, complimenting the first three people you see at school, writing a kind message on a family member's bathroom mirror with a dry erase marker, or bringing flowers to your teacher. Being kind is easy when you get creative!

Benefits

Pay It Forward is a great way to teach children about the benefits of kindness and how it can spread quickly with one simple gesture. The exercise also builds teamwork and planning skills.

What to Say

- As a family, we are going to Pay It Forward. Pay It Forward means we will do random acts of kindness in hopes that it will inspire others to do them as well. We want our kind acts to be contagious, which means we want others to start being kind and doing random acts.
- Let's think of some ideas of kind acts we can do for others. Let's try to come up with four acts that we can all do together as a family. I'll write them down and then we can decide which kind acts to do. Who'd like to share their ideas first?

KINDNESS FORTUNE TELLER

This activity involves creating an origami fortune teller that is filled with kindness activities. Children will enjoy making the Kindness Fortune Teller and have even more fun turning one of their choices into a kind action. Any act of kindness matters—even something as small as a smile can make a difference in someone's life. The Kindness Fortune Teller inspires eight kinds of acts in a fun, engaging manner.

Benefits

Kindness Fortune Teller has multiple steps, which makes it a good activity to enhance executive functioning (e.g., planning, organization, working memory). Origami requires focus and concentration. The actions written inside the fortune teller encourage kindness and connectedness.

What to Say

- We are going to make Kindness Fortune Tellers! Start with the white side up if using origami paper. Fold in half to make a triangle. Open the paper and then fold it in half again, making a triangle. Open the fortune teller flat again.
- Fold each corner into the center point.
- Turn over and again fold each corner into the center point.
- Fold in half along creases, both ways, and open.
- Number each compartment from 1 through 8 on the colored side.
- Open up each flap and write a fortune in each of the eight compartments. For inspiration, here are some kindness fortunes you could use:
    - Leave change with a small kindness note on a vending machine.
    - Name four things you are grateful for today.
    - Say something nice to the next four people you talk to.
    - Hold the door open and greet all who enter with a happy hello.
    - Help clean up.
    - Smile at the next four people you see.

    - Make a thank-you card for someone.
    - Leave happy notes around your house.
    - Turn the model over and write a color on each of the outside flaps.
- Your Kindness Fortune Teller is complete. Use your thumb and index fingers to open it. Ask a friend or family member to pick one of the top four squares. Open and close the fortune teller as you spell out the color your friend chose. Next, have your friend choose a number from the inside flap of the fortune teller. Open and close the fortune teller the amount of the number they picked. Finally, pick another number, open the flap, and let the kind fortunes begin.

Mindfulness Variation

To make the process easier if you're strapped for time, download and print a Kindness Fortune Teller from www.doinggoodtogether.org. Then all you need to do is fold it along the lines.

KINDNESS SCAVENGER HUNT

This activity is great to do as a group, either as a family or a class. Type fifteen kindness and mindfulness activities on your computer, print them out, cut them into strips, and hide them inside plastic Easter eggs. Hide the eggs around your house, classroom, or yoga studio. Have children find the eggs. Ask them to open them one at a time and then do the activity written inside. Here is a list of ideas to place in the eggs:

- Compliment a friend or classmate.
- Send a kind wish to a family member.
- Take three deep Balloon Breaths.
- Hold a Tree Pose for five breaths. Don't forget to switch sides, place your weight on the opposite foot, and take five breaths again.
- Close your eyes and listen for three sounds. What did you hear?
- Find a nonmoving object in the room. Pretend to be that object for ten seconds.
- Close your eyes. Take three Elevator Breaths. Notice your heartbeat and breath.
- Find seven green objects in the room.
- Close your eyes. Notice two sensations in your body (e.g., hunger, warmth, happiness).
- Be a dog for five breaths. Wag your tail—you're a happy dog!
- Relax in Mummy Pose for five breaths. Notice how you feel.
- Send a kind wish to someone who bothers you.
- Send a kind wish to yourself.
- Give this Kindness Coin to someone you see being kind.
- Smile at someone.

Materials

- Plastic Easter eggs
- Paper strips
- Ambient music
- Magnetic wands and chips

Benefits

The Kindness Scavenger Hunt helps children with focus while creating connectedness and community. This activity promotes mindful awareness, kindness, and yoga pose practice.

What to Say

- Let's form a circle. I've hidden ten plastic eggs. I want you each to find two eggs and then return to the circle.
- We will take turns opening the eggs and doing the kind action written on the piece of paper inside. When you hear the music, begin!

Mindfulness Variation

For an extra dose of mindfulness, add magnetic wands and chips. Place two or three magnetic chips in the egg with the kindness statement. Hide the eggs in easy to access places so your child can place the wand over the egg. Your child may have to move the wand over the egg until it connects with the magnet. Once the egg connects with the wand, have your child slowly walk with the wand carrying the egg.

CHAPTER 9

Relaxing and Restoring

Relaxing and restoring integrates several research-backed techniques, including some already covered in this book. The combination of breathing, movement, and mindfulness is powerful and has an immediate effect, helping your child to de-stress. The techniques that are combined in this chapter include the use of ambient music, muscle relaxation, aromatherapy, and deep pressure. Visualization is also an important part of relaxation with children. Guided visualizations release tension and stress, while enhancing creative imagery. Visualization provides a focal point for your child while she is relaxing.

There are important elements that help children relax. Children need to be comfortable both mentally and physically. Roger Cole, PhD, yoga teacher and relaxation physiologist educated at Stanford University, specializes in the science of relaxation. Here are some of the conditions Dr. Cole describes that will enhance your child's relaxation:

- Physical comfort
- Muscle release
- Warmth
- Reclined or inverted position
- Darkness
- Deep breathing

The activities in this chapter will help your child relax, quickly calming the body and mind to reduce stressful situations and experiences. Relaxing and restoring can be helpful in a variety of situations, from daily stressors at school to difficulty falling asleep at night.

Restoring Poses

The mind, movement, and breath are all connected to the relaxation response in the body. Certain poses activate the quieting reflexes of the brain. Children release stress through poses, breathing, and focus of the mind.

SLEEPING BUTTERFLY

Sleeping Butterfly is a restorative yoga pose that helps children relax. In Sleeping Butterfly your child reclines on a bolster or pillow, which allows the hips and the back to open up. It has a soothing effect, which doubles when calming breathing exercises are added to it, such as the ones found in Chapter 3.

Materials

- Bolster or pillows
- Yoga block or thick book

Benefits

Children become aware of and release tension in different parts of their body with breath work and mindfulness. Sleeping Butterfly is a backbend that promotes digestion, a sense of calm, and deep breathing.

What to Say

- We are going to practice being sleeping butterflies. Come to Easy Seated Pose. I'm going to place a pillow behind your back that is on a yoga block to make it recline.
- Let's put some pretend glue on the bottoms of our feet. Gently but firmly move your hands up and down your feet to apply the glue. Now bring the bottoms of your feet together.
- Lie down on your pillow. Let's place an eye pillow over our eyes to help our butterflies sleep more soundly. Would you like one on your feet as well? Take a deep breath in through your nose. As you release your breath, let your body melt into the pillow.
- Let's take ten more Elevator Breaths (Chapter 3). Engage your mindful butterfly senses and notice how you feel.

LEGS UP THE WALL

This exercise feels silly, but is very beneficial! Legs Up the Wall is considered a restorative pose in yoga that is soothing to the back. It is typically done toward the end of class as a transition into relaxation.

Materials

- Small pillows or bolsters

Benefits

This restorative yoga pose has a relaxing effect on the nervous system. It is a great pose for children who are on their feet or sitting a lot, as it recirculates the blood in the legs.

What to Say

- Let's sit as close as possible to the wall. Turn sideways and pretend that your hip is glued to the wall. Bend your knees. Slowly turn and lie on your back while still keeping your hip glued to the wall, so your tail is right against the wall. Stretch your legs long so they go up the wall.
- I'm going to place a small pillow under your hips and head. Scoot forward as needed to move your tailbone so it is touching the wall. Find a comfortable position for your arms. Would you like a blanket? Take a deep breath in through your nose. Notice your body in the pose. What does it feel like to have your legs up the wall? Let your breath out.
- Continue to notice how you feel. After ten deep breaths, bend your knees and roll to your side. Slowly come up to a seated position. Notice how you feel.

CORPSE POSE

Corpse Pose is the final relaxation pose in most yoga classes. It is similar to Mummy Pose (Chapter 2), but the children's arms are relaxed alongside their bodies with palms facing up. Corpse Pose is a great pose for children to find inner peace and calm.

Benefits

Corpse is a relaxing pose that releases stress and tension.

What to Say

- We are going to relax in Corpse Pose. Lie on your back with your arms at your sides. Relax your arms and have your palms facing up. Close your eyes.
- As you breathe in, feel your belly rise, and as you breathe out, feel it fall. Let's take nine more breaths. Ah...feels good!

SLEEPING CHILD

Sleeping Child is a restorative pose that helps children relax. Sleeping Child requires the use of a bolster or pillow and a yoga block to build a slight incline. Place a yoga block or thick book under the top of the bolster or pillow.

Materials

- Yoga bolster or pillow
- Yoga block or thick book

Benefits

Sleeping Child supports digestion as it gently massages the abdominal organs. Sleeping Child helps children relax and release stress and promotes inner peace and a sense of calm.

What to Say

- I've placed this yoga pillow on a block for you. Let's sit right behind it with our knees wide on either side of the low end of the pillow. Gently lie on the pillow, resting your entire belly on it, so you feel comfortable. Turn your head to one side. Take a deep breath in through your nose, making your belly rise against the pillow. Notice how you feel. Release your breath.
- Let's take nine deep breaths. Ah...feels good. Slowly turn your head to the other side. Take ten deep breaths on this side. Gently come to a sitting position. How do you feel?

TRANQUIL TWIST

Twists are known for their ability to tone and cleanse the body. Reclined twists can soothe the nerves and leave your child feeling rested and restored. Tranquil Twist is a restorative yoga pose that serves as a transition pose to final relaxation in yoga classes.

Benefits

Tranquil Twist is calming to the nervous system. It reduces stress and tension and feels good. It increases range of motion. Tranquil Twist eases back and neck tension. It improves digestion and opens the lungs.

What to Say

- Let's lie on our backs. Bend your knees and give them a big hug. Stretch your arms out. Let your knees drop to one side. Keep your shoulder glued to the ground. Turn your head in the other direction.
- Take ten deep Counting Breaths (Chapter 3). Bring your knees back to center. Let them drop to the other side.
- Turn your head in the opposite direction of your knees. Close your eyes. Take ten deep Counting Breaths (Chapter 3).

Relaxation Stories

To practice relaxing in yoga, an adult lies on his mat at the end of the class, closing his eyes and focusing on his breath. But this approach to relaxation doesn't work well with children. After all, they are used to being entertained by electronic devices. Relaxation stories help children achieve a feeling of calm by infusing stories with sensory experiences they can feel, imagine, and smell. These stories also incorporate progressive relaxation of body parts into the story. Visual images, movement, and sense of smell are used to increase the feelings of calm and relaxation.

RAINFOREST RELAXATION

Rainforest Relaxation is a relaxation story that is infused with mindful movement, progressive relaxation, and aromatherapy to entertain children and engage multiple senses. Rainforest Relaxation teaches children to breathe deeply, reduce muscle tension, and visualize.

Materials

- Cotton balls
- Therapeutic-grade essential oils (orange, lime, lemon, grapefruit)

Benefits

Mindfulness helps children create space between how they feel and how they react. It teaches your child to deal with strong emotions more calmly. Rainforest Relaxation decreases stress and helps children relax while promoting mindful awareness and inner peace.

What to Say

- Lie down comfortably on your back. Close your eyes and take in three deep Elevator Breaths (Chapter 3). Feel the ground underneath you and begin to relax.
- Place a hand on your heart and one on your belly. Notice your heartbeat and your breath.
- Imagine that you are lying on raft. The raft is filled with beautiful pillows that are soft and feel good to lie on. Breathe in and out through your nose, feeling

your belly rise on the in-breath and fall on the out-breath. Imagine yourself floating down a river deep in the rainforest. The warm sun is shining and you can feel its rays touching your face. The breeze is blowing in your hair. You feel relaxed floating down this calm, peaceful river.

- Now picture the rainforest in your mind, the beautiful flowers and vines in a rainbow of colors, the tall, magnificent trees. Listen closely. Can you hear the birds singing? What else do you hear? Do you hear the water flowing faster? There are a few rapids ahead. If you would like to feel the rapids move your raft, raise your hand. Make your body straight and stiff. Curl your hands into fists and scrunch up your face. Notice how you feel.
- Now I'll place my hands around your ankles, pull gently, and sway your legs back and forth as if you are floating over rapids in the water. Next, I'll gently place your feet and legs back on the ground. The rapids are gone; take a deep breath in, and as you release it let your body relax into your raft.
- Relax your fingers and toes. Relax your face, moving your jaw back and forth slowly. Notice how you feel just floating calmly down the river.
- Alongside the river are big, majestic trees covered in rainforest fruits, such as grapefruits, lemons, limes, and oranges. The fruits smell amazing as you travel under the trees in your raft. If you would like to smell the fruit, raise your hand. (Place a drop of lemon, grapefruit, lime, or orange therapeutic-grade essential oil on a cotton ball and place the cotton ball in your child's hand.) Continue to breathe deeply, smelling the fruit on the trees above. Notice what the fruit reminds you of and how it makes you feel. Take a few moments to appreciate all the good things in your life.
- Slowly rise up to Easy Seated Pose (Chapter 2). Notice how you feel.

MINDFUL BUTTERFLY MEDITATION

The Mindful Butterfly Meditation helps entertain your child while exploring relaxation and stress-management exercises. This mindfulness meditation is simple and fun, and you and your child can practice together. This meditation teaches children that being brave and facing their fears can make them feel happier.

Materials

- Aerial yoga hammock, regular hammock, or yoga mat
- Ambient nature sounds
- Cotton balls
- Lime therapeutic-grade essential oil

Benefits

Teaching children mindfulness strengthens their attention and ability to self-regulate. When children imagine themselves doing something a little scary successfully the likelihood for taking part in the behavior increases. Active imagination reduces anxiety and depression. It builds positive attitudes, feelings, and behavior.

What to Say

- Let's lie on our back either on the floor or in your hammock. Take three Elevator Breaths (Chapter 3). Imagine that you are a caterpillar and the hammock is your cocoon. Your cocoon is hanging from the branch of a big, sturdy tree.
- Draw your attention to your breath. Breathe in and out slowly through your nose. Begin to notice the sensations around you. Is the wind gently rocking your cocoon, are birds singing...what do you notice? There is a creek gurgling near your tree; can you hear it? Your caterpillar has been working very hard. He had to climb the big tree, eat lots of leaves, and spin a cocoon.
- All this work has made him very stressed out. Make your body tight like a stressed caterpillar wrapped snugly in a cocoon. Notice what you feel. As you take a deep breath in, notice how it feels to breathe when your body is tight. Pause. As you release your breath, relax your entire body. Feel your arms and

legs becoming heavier, and more deeply relaxed; feel your body become heavy and sink into your cocoon. Feel your shoulders become loose and droopy. Take in a deep breath and as you let it out, make your body calm and relaxed.

- As your body relaxes it begins to transform. Your droopy shoulders become wings, curly antennae sprout from your head, and you are transformed into a beautiful butterfly. Picture the color of your butterfly in your mind. Does it have stripes or spots?
- As your butterfly emerges from his cocoon, he finds himself on a branch high in the air. He no longer has legs to walk down the tree and he is a little afraid of jumping off the branch, as he has never flown before. Take a deep breath in, then slowly blow out any fears your butterfly may be feeling. Breathe in again and repeat to yourself, "I am brave." Take in three more breaths as you repeat to yourself, "I am brave."
- Imagine your brave butterfly taking flight off the branch. As you soar through the air, you feel happy that you were brave and flew off the branch. The land below you is full of colors and amazing sights you couldn't see as a caterpillar.
- Floating through the air is peaceful and the air smells sweet, like fruit. You notice a grove of trees covered in green fruit and softly land on the fruit. If you would like to smell the sweet scent of the fruit, raise your hand. (Place a cotton ball with a half-drop of therapeutic-grade lime oil in your child's hand.) Take ten deep breaths, smelling the fruit.
- Afterward, slowly rise to Easy Seated Pose. Notice how you feel. Can anyone describe times when you needed to be brave to accomplish something? How did you feel before this activity and after it?

Mindfulness Variation

To encourage your child to stay still and quiet during the Mindful Butterfly Meditation, tell her to be very still so a butterfly can land on her. Place a plastic butterfly on her belly.

LOTUS FLOWER

The Lotus Flower is thought to symbolize beauty, grace, love, and perseverance, which makes it a wonderful theme for a relaxation script for children. The Lotus Flower rises from muddy waters every morning to bloom into a beautiful flower. This progressive relaxation activity mimics the lotus rising from the muddy water into the bright sunlight.

Materials

- Cotton balls
- Lavender therapeutic-grade essential oil

Benefits

The Lotus Flower builds children's imagination. It enhances relaxation and focus while decreasing stress and building self-esteem.

What to Say

- Imagine that you are a tiny seed. Make your body small and tight just like a seed. Bring your knees into your chest. Curl your hands into fists and curl your toes under. Bring your shoulders up by your ears and scrunch your face up. Notice how it feels to be small and tight. Close your eyes.
- Your seed is buried in murky, muddy water. Take a deep breath in and fill your seed with air. As you breathe out, imagine that your body is a long stem stretching and growing to the surface of the water. Relax your arms and your legs and stretch them out long.
- Bring your arms alongside your body and let your stem relax. Your stem has to stay flexible and relaxed or else it will break and your flower will not bloom above the muddy waters. I'm going to come by and do the stem test on you to make sure your stem is completely relaxed. (Pick up your child's ankles and move her body back and forth.) Ah...what a wonderfully relaxed stem. (Now gently set down your child's ankles.)
- Now feel your flower bursting through the top of the muddy waters. Your petals slowly open and you feel the sun on them. Take a deep breath in through your nose. Let it out. Imagine yourself as a beautiful Lotus Flower sitting on top of

the muddy water. See the color of your petals. You are not dirty from the mud, but are beautiful and smell wonderful.

- If you would like to smell the peaceful scent of your flower, raise your hand. (Place a cotton ball with a half-drop of lavender essential oil in the child's hand.) As you breathe in, fill your body with light. As you breathe out, imagine dark, stale air leaving your body. Take ten counting breaths.
- Now the sun is setting and your petals are folding in. Your Lotus Flower becomes a bud again and begins to sink back to the bottom of the pond. Take a deep breath in. Let it out. Slowly rise to a seated position. Notice how you feel.

MAGIC CARPET RIDE

Children embrace fun interactive stories that engage all of their senses. Magic Carpet Ride is a relaxation story that weaves in thinking positive thoughts and reflecting on good memories to improve mood. Relaxation stories introduce your child to meditation and mindfulness.

Materials

- Aerial hammock, hammock, or yoga mat
- Cotton balls
- Orange therapeutic-grade essential oil
- Ambient music

Benefits

Progressive relaxation improves attention, concentration, behavior, and self-concept. Mindfulness meditations in general reduce anxiety, tension, and heart rate. Magic Carpet Ride quiets the mind and promotes inner peace and better sleep.

What to Say

- Lie comfortably on your back. Take a deep breath in through your nose. Fill your belly with air and release it. Continue to breathe in and out through your nose, feeling yourself relax.

- Imagine that you are lying on a magic carpet. Your magic carpet plays relaxing, peaceful music. Listen to the rhythm and continue to breathe in and out through your nose. Feel your muscles relax as your magic carpet begins to float into the air. See yourself lying on the magic carpet that is filled with soft pillows. Imagine your body sinking into the pillows as you become more relaxed and calm.
- It is nighttime so the sky is dark and filled with stars and a bright, full moon. The stars twinkle and are beautiful to watch. This gives you a peaceful feeling. Breathe in deeply and slowly.
- However, the wind begins to pick up. Suddenly, your magic carpet begins to experience windy conditions, which causes you to make your body stiff and tight like a board. Notice how tight your muscles feel. (Gently, but firmly, grab your child's ankles, pull gently, and then rock her side to side. Then, set her ankles down.) Ah, the wind is settled down. Take a deep breath in. Let all your breath out and relax your body back into your fluffy pillows.
- Imagine that your magic carpet is taking you to your most favorite place on Earth. It could be your grandmother's house, the library, beach, or even Disney World. Notice how thinking about your favorite place makes you feel. Take a deep breath in and then let it out.
- Pretend your carpet has arrived at your special place. Experience the sights, sounds, and sensations of your favorite place.
- Now feel your carpet begin to rise again into the air. As you are floating through the air, you notice the smell of oranges. You look down from your magic carpet and see a grove of orange trees. You're so close you can almost touch the oranges. You reach out your hand and grab one as you are floating by. What does the orange feel like? What does the orange look like in the moonlight? Imagine what it would taste like. If you'd like to smell the orange, raise your hand. (Put half a drop of orange essential oil on a cotton ball and put it in your child's hand.) Continue to breathe slowly and deeply.
- Now your magic carpet has reached its destination. Take a deep breath in and sigh it out through your mouth. Slowly rise to a seated position. Notice how you feel.

SUNKEN TREASURE

Sunken Treasure is a relaxation story for children that combines gentle calming movement, breathing, progressive relaxation, and aromatherapy. This multisensory meditation engages the brain and induces the relaxation response to reduce stress and tension.

Materials

- Cotton balls
- Cedarwood therapeutic-grade essential oil

Benefits

Progressive relaxation helps children recognize the difference between tension and relaxation in their muscles. It will also help your child improve focus and be receptive to learning, because the mind works more effectively when it is relaxed.

What to Say

- Lie on your back in a comfortable position. Close your eyes. Imagine that you are a fish swimming through the ocean. Slowly move your body side to side, like a fish swimming through the ocean. Feel the warm water all around you giving you a great big hug. Breathe in through your nose. Breathe out through your nose.
- Now imagine that the sky is turning dark and it is starting to rain. The big waves are a little scary for your fish, so he swims deeper into the ocean, looking for a place to hide from the storm. He spots a tiny rock cave. Make your body small and tight so you can fit into the rock cave. Squeeze your hands into fists, curl your toes under, and scrunch up your face. Become a tight little ball. Notice how tight your muscles feel. Keep breathing in through your nose and out through your nose. Feel the waves rocking back and forth in the cave. Rock your body side to side and back and forth on your back.
- The storm passes and the sun begins to shine through the water. Take a deep breath in, filling up with air. Imagine you are breathing in a ray of sunshine and send it all the way to your toes. As you breathe out, let the dark storm out, stretch out your legs and arms. Wiggle your fingers and toes. Let your body relax into the ocean. Just float. In your mind, say, "I am relaxed."

- As your fish is floating and relaxing, he sees a shape down deep in the water. Very slowly, he begins to swim deeper to investigate. When he gets closer he smells wood and realizes it is a very old sunken pirate ship. If you would like to smell the wood from the pirate ship, raise your hand. (Place half a drop of cedarwood essential oil, which has a woodsy and earthy smell to it, on a cotton ball and wave it slowly under your child's nose.) Your fish begins to explore the ship and finds a treasure chest filled with gold coins and jewels. Imagine what the treasure chest looks like in your mind. What colors are the jewels? Do they sparkle? What do they feel like? Take a deep breath in. Let it out.
- Your fish is becoming tired so he closes his eyes. He feels the waves gently rocking him back and forth. He can hear the waves of the ocean above him and it is relaxing.
- Take in one more deep breath, filling up with sunshine again. Let it all out. Slowly rise to a seated position.

BODY SCANNER

Body Scanner is similar to an X-ray machine in that the body is scanned, but instead of looking for broken bones, this imaginary scanner is looking for stress, tension, and tightness. Body Scanner is a classic mindfulness meditation from the adult Mindfulness-Based Stress Reduction program. This version has been adapted for children. The goal of exercises like Body Scanner is to draw your child's attention inward by directing attention to each part of her body during the relaxation story.

Benefits

Body Scanner teaches your child body awareness and mindful awareness. It is relaxing and calming to the nervous system, so it reduces stress and tension. Body Scanner also increases attention, concentration, and focus.

What to Say

- Lie on your back in Mummy Pose. Fill your belly up with air as if you are inflating a balloon. Breathe out and feel the balloon deflate.
- Imagine that you are lying in a magical machine that can scan your body for stress and tension. This special machine needs your help to figure out which parts of the body are tight. As it moves over the different body parts, try hard to focus on the areas the machine is scanning. Ready?
- The machine is scanning your head. Notice how your hair feels. What about your ears? How does your face feel?
- Now the machine moves to your shoulders. Are your shoulders relaxed or stiff and tight? Are they up by your ears or falling down your back? Send a big deep breath to your shoulders. Feel your shoulder muscles relax and let go.
- The machine is scanning your arms and hands. What do they feel like? Are your hands in fists or loose and wiggly? Take a deep breath in and send it to your arms and hands. Feel them become heavy and relaxed.
- The scanner is moving over your hips. What do you notice about your hips? Take a mindful breath in and send it all the way down to your hips. Can you feel your hips stretch out as you breathe in? Let your breath out slowly.

- Your legs are being scanned. Are your legs stiff like boards? Breathe in all the way down to your feet. Breathe out, feeling your legs become heavy and relaxed like cooked spaghetti noodles.
- We've reached your toes. What is the scanner telling us about your toes? Are they tight and curled under or loose and spread out? Take a deep breath in and see if you can send it all the way to your pinky toes.
- The Body Scanner is done! You have calmed your body and your mind. Take a deep breath in. Let it out. Notice how you feel.

SQUEEZE IT

Squeeze It is a progressive muscle relaxation activity that your child can use anytime and anywhere. Make it fun by turning it into a game!

Materials

- Chime (available inexpensively online)

Benefits

Releasing tension helps children to feel relaxed and calm. Squeeze It increases body awareness and mindful awareness.

What to Say

- Let's play a relaxation game called Squeeze It, but first let's get our minds and bodies ready. Lie comfortably on the floor. Place one hand on your heart and one hand on your tummy. Notice your heartbeat and your breath. Are they slow, medium, or fast? Begin to breathe deeply, feeling your hands rise and fall. Feel yourself relaxing with each breath.
- I'm going to ring the chime. Let's take long, slow, deep breaths until we can't hear it any longer. Place your finger on your nose when you can't hear it anymore. Great!
- We are ready to play Squeeze It. Bring your arms to your sides like Corpse Pose. As you take a breath in, curl your toes into a ball. Tighten up your whole foot. Hold it and notice how it feels. As you breathe out, release your toes. One more time. Deep breath in, curl your toes super tight. Hold it and notice how it feels. As you breathe out, relax your toes. Wiggle your toes and let them relax. Ah...feels good!
- Let's squeeze our hands. Take a deep breath in. Make your hands into fist and squeeze it tight. Pause and notice how it feels. Release your breath and your fingers. Relax and wiggle them. One last time, breathe in and make a fist. Pause and squeeze it tighter. Breathe out and let your fingers relax.
- Let's take a couple deep breaths in and out through the nose. Notice how you feel. Slowly rise up to a seated position. Ah...feels good!

Thought Watching

Mindfulness entails being aware of your thoughts and feelings, but not engaging with them—just noticing them. Thought-watching exercises are a simple way to teach children this concept.

CLOUD WATCHING

Thoughts are similar to clouds—they come and go. Cloud Watching helps children build awareness of their thoughts. They watch their thoughts as they are happening and then let them go without engaging them. Cloud Watching is a fun way to teach children that thoughts can float past without having to think about them, just like a cloud. When children increase their awareness of their thoughts and allow themselves to be present, they begin to relax.

Materials

- Paper
- Colored pencils

Benefits

Cloud Watching increases awareness and teaches children to be still. It also enhances attention, focus, and relaxation. Cloud Watching increases mindful awareness.

What to Say

- Let's lie down comfortably on our backs. Close your eyes. Imagine that you are lying in the grass, looking up at a clear blue sky. Begin to engage in Elevator Breath (Chapter 3). Notice your breath and heartbeat. Begin to make the breath slower and longer.
- We are going to pretend that our minds are the blue sky and that our thoughts are the clouds. Let's simply pay attention to the clouds or thoughts that float by. Watch the clouds as they form and let them float on by. Allow the wind to gently carry them away. Remember, we are just watching them. Notice their shape and how they move. Continue to breathe deeply in and out through the nose, watching your clouds for one minute.

- Slowly rise up to a seated position. Let's draw a picture of the sky and clouds you saw in your mind. If you like, you can draw a face on the cloud to show the emotion of the thought or cloud, or you can name the cloud. What did you notice? Was it hard to let the clouds just float by?

Mindfulness Variation

Have your child practice thought-watching for a week. After each Cloud Watching session, have them draw their clouds and keep a Cloud Watching journal. Write down any changes they notice, such as if fewer clouds appear or maybe the clouds move at a slower speed. Also, have them write down their mood and notice how it affects the cloudy sky.

Mindful Meditations

The following meditations involve children watching something that moves slowly and calmly, or engaging the tactile sense while breathing and being mindful. This practice allows children to notice things they may not have noticed before. The movement is soothing to the nervous system and initiates feelings of relaxation. Your child can watch or touch the object while taking deep, calming breaths.

FALLING BUBBLES

In this meditation, children pay close attention to the experience of mindful seeing. Falling Bubbles requires the use of a Liquid Motion Bubbler, which can be purchased inexpensively online. Falling Bubbles is a sight meditation that has a soothing and calming effect. Your child will find a comfortable position and watch the slow rhythmic drops the bubbler provides while taking deep breaths.

Materials

- Liquid Motion Bubbler

Benefits

Falling Bubbles provides simple visual stimulation that is calming and centering. Falling Bubbles helps children reduce hyperactivity and learn to focus and relax. It relieves stress and tension.

What to Say

- Let's find a comfortable position, such as Easy Seated Pose, Corpse Pose, or Cobra Pose. Focus your eyes on the bubbler. Breathe in, filling up with air. Breathe out, releasing all the air. Continue to breathe slowly and calmly.
- Try to keep as still as you can, watching the bubbler, until all the bubbles are at the bottom. Yay! You did it! Let's turn it over and try it again.

SETTLE YOUR GLITTER

Settle Your Glitter is a mindfulness activity that is used to help children center and relax. Children love to make their own bottle and choose their own colors of glitter. Fill a clear plastic bottle with hot water, a tablespoon of glycerin, and a drop of liquid dish soap. Have your child choose three different colors of glitter. Pick one color to represent feelings, one to represent thoughts, and one to represent behavior. Sprinkle each color into the plastic bottle using a funnel.

Materials

- Glitter
- Hot water
- Dish soap
- Glycerin
- Funnel

Benefits

A mindfulness bottle is a fun visual prop to teach children how deep breathing can calm the body and the mind. The mindfulness bottle gives children a tool to calm down and focus their minds (settle their glitter) before they make a decision.

What to Say

- We're going to make glitter bottles. The glitter represents our thoughts, feelings, and behaviors. When we are upset, nervous, or mad, our glitter is unsettled. What can you do to settle your glitter?
- Start by finding a comfortable position.
- Let's go one by one, sharing an event that was difficult for some reason (such as giving a speech in front of your class, losing a sports game, watching a scary movie).
- Shake the glitter bottle. When you are upset, your thoughts are chaotic, which means your feelings and urges are out of control, just like the glitter.
- Set the bottle in front of you. Take ten deep breaths in and out through your nose. Feel your belly rise on the inhale and fall on the exhale.
- Do your best to focus your attention on your breath. While you breathe, watch the glitter float down and settle on the bottom of the jar, just like our thoughts. Take a moment each day to practice settling your glitter.

ORBEEZ MEDITATION

Orbeez Meditation is a calming touch meditation. Orbeez or water beads start off as small, hard balls, but when you add water, they grow more than one hundred times their size and become wet, soft, and squishy. This provides the ultimate soothing meditation for children. This activity might not be suitable for young children who like to put small objects in their mouths. This meditation takes a little prep time. Parents will need to soak the beads overnight to allow them time to grow.

Materials

- Orbeez or water beads
- Small plastic tub
- Water
- Calming ambient music

Benefits

The soft and soothing texture of the Orbeez is calming to children. This meditation activity builds tactile discrimination and creative exploration.

What to Say

- Let's relax with Orbeez today. Sit down in front of the tub of Orbeez and get comfortable. Place your hands in the tub. Close your eyes. Begin to breathe deeply in through your nose and out through your nose.
- Gently move your hands in the tub, noticing how the Orbeez feel. Are they wet or dry? Do they feel hard or soft? Just notice, without labeling how they feel.
- Let's add another sense. Notice what sounds you hear as you move your hands in the Orbeez. Now take one Orbeez in your hand and bring it up to your nose. Remember, we are just noticing. We are not labeling it as bad or good. What does it smell like? Gently place it back in the tub.
- Let's open our eyes. What do you see? I'm going to play music while you notice the Orbeez with all of your senses.

PART THREE

Putting It All Together

Neuroscience shows us that implementing a practice of mindfulness for as little as ten minutes a day can change the structure of the brain. That translates to improved grades, enhanced self-regulation, and happier children. The positive effects of mindfulness are limitless in the long term when it comes to taking mindfulness off the mat and into the world.

Mindfulness, or paying attention with the senses, improves how your child's brain and body function, by helping him to build awareness and slow down. By building mindful awareness, your child is able to be less reactive. Your child will reflect before responding. The awareness that mindfulness promotes allows your child to pick healthier coping mechanisms. Secondly, your child slows down. When in a mindful state, your child's body goes into relaxation mode. As he relaxes, he can think clearer, which leads to wiser decisions and a healthy, resilient child.

CHAPTER 10

Mindfulness Off the Mat

This final chapter will help you put together all you have learned to create a practice of mindfulness. Being mindful is an ongoing process or lifestyle; it is not an isolated activity. It takes practice just like any other skill. Your child will not master it overnight, but with practice, when things are running smoothly, your child will be able to draw upon his mindfulness skills and use them to de-stress.

At this point, you may be wondering, "But how do I develop a mindfulness practice for my child?" This final section will provide some basic sequences that you can use for certain situations, and information on how to create your own sequences using the information in this book. These are only guidelines, not rules, drawing on knowledge from research and personal experience. You know your child best and can create a practice that benefits your family's unique needs. By the end of this section you should have all the tools you need to live a more mindful life that supports compassion and awareness.

Sequencing Mindfulness Activities

The science of mindfulness shows us that while the individual activities in this book are powerfully beneficial to your child's brain and body, they are even more powerful when combined together to form a sequence. If possible combine items from each of the eight chapters together to create a comprehensive mindfulness practice for your child. The chapter topics are movement, breathing, senses, eating, focus, positive affirmations, kindness/gratitude, and relaxing. You will notice that the activities move back and forth from high-energy activities to low-energy activities; this is done purposefully to engage attention and to teach self-regulation. A basic children's mindfulness practice should include activities from several of the chapters as follows:

- **Mindful Movement.** Many children spend too much time sitting and not enough time moving. When children move in an integrated manner, full brain activation occurs. Create a Mindful Jungle Course (Chapter 2), play Crab Soccer (Chapter 6), or have a Mind-Set Dance Party (Chapter 7) to get them moving.
- **Proprioceptive Exercises.** These are important for focus and attention; provide these activities before doing mindful awareness activities that require sustained concentration. These could include Thunderstorm, Crash Pad, or The Wall Is Falling (Chapter 4).
- **Mindful Breathing, Focus, and Eating.** Next, choose one activity from each of the breathing, focus, and eating chapters. Now that your child has moved and gotten the wiggles out, she should be able to cultivate mindful awareness.
- **Mindfulness and the Senses.** This is where you will begin to transition children into relaxation. Activities from Chapter 4, such as Finding Sounds, Ambient Music, or Chime Listening work well here.
- **Relaxation.** Choose one of the relaxation stories and pair it with one of the restoring poses from Chapter 8.
- **Reflection.** End your mindfulness practice with a reflection. As with all mindfulness activities, reflect on the experience with your child. This will broaden your awareness of what activities resonated with your child and help to guide your future sequences.

Sample Sequences

The following sequences have been provided to demonstrate how to put different activities together to create a themed sequence. The benefits listed for each activity along with the sequencing tips can help you to build your own sequences for you and your child to do together.

Reducing Worries and Stress with Mindfulness

Children today are faced with many stressors, such as friends, homework, school, and inadequate sleep. This sequence of mindfulness activities emphasizes stress reduction to create a sense of calmness, while enhancing mindful awareness, focus, and executive functioning.

What to Say

- Let's begin with a Mind-Set Dance Party (Chapter 7). Before we begin, lie in Corpse Pose (Chapter 9). Close your eyes, place one hand on your heart and one on your lower belly. Notice your heartbeat and breath. Take in three Elevator Breaths (Chapter 3).
- Slowly rise to a seated position. I'm going to put on some music (play a growth mind-set song). Move your body, dance, and sing. Notice how your body feels. Be free and have fun! Great dancing and singing!
- Come to an Easy Seated Pose (Chapter 2), place one hand on your heart and one on your lower belly. Notice your heartbeat and breath. Did they change? Notice how you feel.
- Now I'm going to play some ambient music while we practice Breathing with Bubbles (Chapter 3). Take a deep breath in through your nose and release it slowly. Remember, breathe long and slow.
- Let's practice our mindfulness skills while eating these apple slices by Eating Mindfully (Chapter 5).
- Using our mindfulness bottles, let's practice Settle Your Glitter (Chapter 9). Shake up your jar to unsettle your glitter, then let's settle it with Tranquil Twist (Chapter 9). Hold Tranquil Twist for five breaths in this direction, now switch to the other side for five breaths. Notice how you feel.

- Lie down in Corpse Pose (Chapter 9). Lie comfortably on your back with your arms along the sides of your body. We are going to do some mindfulness with Chime Listening (Chapter 4) and Counting Breaths (Chapter 3). Remember to listen with all of your senses. When you hear the chime, listen as long and carefully as you can. When you can't hear the chime any longer place a hand on your heart and show me how many counting breaths you took while listening, keep your eyes closed. Great mindfulness!
- Let's be Sleeping Butterflies (Chapter 9). Place the soles of your feet together and lie back on the bolster. Place on one hand on your heart and one on your lower belly and take ten deep breaths.
- Now lie down in Mummy Pose (Chapter 2) for our relaxation story. Our relaxation story is Mindful Butterfly Meditation (Chapter 9). If you would like an eye pillow for your butterfly, bring your finger to your nose and I will put one on your eyes. Let's begin.

Reducing High Energy Levels

Children who are active require mindfulness activities that move a little quicker and are engaging to multiple senses. This sequence is infused with heavy work activities to give children the input they need to be able to benefit from mindfulness activities that focus on the breath and relaxation.

- I've created a Mindful Jungle Course (Chapter 2) for you. I've added a Crash Pad (Chapter 4) to our course and the Hot Chocolate Breath brain challenge (Chapter 3). Remember to move mindfully and slowly through the obstacle course. When you hear the music, you can begin (play ambient music)!
- Let's make a Bubble Mountain (Chapter 3)! Put your straw in the water. Remember to only blow out through the straw. Don't suck in. Take a deep breath in through the nose and then let it out slowly through the mouth. Keep making your mountain grow taller. Fantastic breathing!
- It's mandala-making time! *Mandala* is from Sanskrit, the language of yoga, and means "circle." It means we are united or connected. We are going to make a mandala from this dough (Mandala Dough, Chapter 5). Let's begin in Easy Seated Pose (Chapter 2) and take a couple of deep Balloon Breaths (Chapter 3). Pick up

a piece of the Play-Doh. What does it smell like? Can you identify what it is made of? Does our dough make a sound? What does it feel like? Let's make our mandala. First, we need to make a big circle to frame our mandala. Now that we have our outline you can roll, pat, and shape your dough into your very own mandala.

- I think The Wall Is Falling (Chapter 4). Run! We need to hold it up. Press your hands against the wall. Spread your fingers wide so you can hold up the wall. Use your strength and push! Okay, I think it's solid now. We can let go. Ah... that was hard work!
- We are going to explore this kinetic sand mindfully (Kinetic Sand Messages, Chapter 8), find some hidden messages, and then create something. Let's begin by being mindful. Remember that being mindful means that we pay attention to something with all of our senses. Great mindfulness. Let's look for the hidden messages and respond to the messages. Fantastic job! You have so many things to be grateful for in your life. Go ahead and create one of the things we talked about and I will try to guess what it is.
- We are going on a Gratitude Hunt (Chapter 8)! We are going in search of the mysterious Gratitude Tree. Let's start our journey by army crawling through these logs that are crossing the river. Next, we are going to jog through the jungle. Start to jog. I see a cobra; he won't bother us if he thinks we are a snake. Plant your feet, make a big balloon with your hands, and pop it all the way to the ground. Come up into Cobra Pose (Chapter 2). Take a deep breath in. Let it out in a "hisss." Two more times. Begin to jog again. I see a lion. We have to make him think we are lions too. Plant your feet, make a big balloon with your hands, and pop it all the way to the ground. Do Lion's Pose with three big Lion's Breaths (Chapter 3). Fantastic, lions! Start to jog again. We are at the end of the jungle—hurray! I think I see the Gratitude Tree ahead, but it is still really far away. Let's ride our Yoga Bicycles (Chapter 2). Oh, no, what is this...a sticky swamp! Slowly walk through the sticky swampy water. We made it! Pick up a leaf off the ground underneath the Gratitude Tree. Let's form a circle and read the leaves we picked up off the ground. Take ten Balloon Breaths (Chapter 3) as you think about what is written on your leaf. Notice how you feel.
- Now lie on your back in a comfortable position, such as Corpse Pose (Chapter 9) or Mummy Pose (Chapter 2). We are going to do a relaxation called Sunken Treasure (Chapter 9).

Focus-Building Sequence

This sequence includes activities that are brain building to promote focus. Use this sequence to balance high energy levels or as a precursor to activities such as homework that require extended concentration. This sequence is a little longer, but can be shortened by taking out Kindness Fortune Teller (Chapter 8) and doing "Hello, Sunshine" (Chapter 2) only one time.

What to Say

- We are going to do "Hello, Sunshine"! Start in Mountain Pose (Chapter 2). Take a big breath in and let it out.
- As you take a deep breath in, grow your mountain by stretching your arms up high above your head. Keep your hands together to make the mountain peak.
- As you breathe out, keep your palms together as you slowly fold forward (Forward Fold, Chapter 2), bending your knees. Bring your hands to the ground in front of you, keeping your palms flat.
- Come up halfway for Monkey Pose (Chapter 2). Bring your hands back to the ground in front of you. Bend your knees. Plant your hands.
- Step one leg back as far as you can, and then the other. Push back through your heels, keeping your legs straight. You are in Plank Pose (Chapter 2).
- Slowly lower all the way to the floor. Take a big breath in and lift your head and heart up as you hiss a long breath out. This is Cobra Pose (Chapter 2).
- Push slowly back up to Plank Pose (knees up or down). Tuck your toes under and lift your tail high for Down Dog Pose (Chapter 2). Hold here for a few breaths.
- As you breathe out, look forward at your hands, bend your knees, and hop or walk both feet forward toward your hands and squat down like a frog. Then raise your tail up for Forward Fold pose.
- Take a deep breath in as you come up halfway for Monkey Pose. Bring your hands back to the ground in front of you. Knees bent. Plant your hands.
- Deep breath in as you straighten your legs, sweep your arms wide as you stand with hands above your head with palms together. Mountain Pose. Let all your breath out as you bring your hands down to your heart center.

- Take a deep breath in. As you release your breath say, "Hello, sunshine!" This completes "Hello, Sunshine."
- Let's come to Easy Seated Pose to practice Brain Breath (Chapter 3).
- Did you know breathing through one nostril can change how you feel? Let's try it. Sit up tall in Easy Seated Pose. Gently place your peace fingers (your pointer and middle fingers) on either side of your nose. Use your right pointer finger to close your right nostril. Breathe in and out slowly and deeply through your left nostril for three breaths. Notice how you feel. Now switch to the other side, closing off your left nostril. Breathe in slowly for three breaths. Notice how you feel.
- We are going to make a Fruit Caterpillar (Chapter 5). Pick pieces of fruit from these bowls. Thread the fruit onto the skewer. Can you make a pattern? Listen to the music and be mindful while making your caterpillar. Notice what you see, hear, smell, and taste. Eat your caterpillar while slowly noticing each bite. What did eating silently and mindfully feel like? Did you notice anything that you haven't noticed before?
- Let's Find the Yoga Joes (Chapter 4). Yoga Joes like to hide when they do yoga. Your job is to find the Yoga Joe and do the pose with him. Then place him back in his studio with his friends. We are going to take three deep breaths in through the nose and out through the nose with each Yoga Joe we find. Ready? Go.
- Now let's make a Kindness Fortune Teller (Chapter 8). Great focus making your fortune teller!
- Let's make the Brain Power Mudra (Chapter 7)! Sit in Easy Seated Pose (Chapter 2). Raise your hands to your heart center and have your palms face each other. Bend your fingers a little and join the tips of the fingers on both hands together. This is the tricky part. Look up with only your eyes. Place your tongue on your top gums as you breathe in and let if fall down as you breathe out.
- We are going to practice relaxing with a relaxation story. Lie down on your back in Corpse Pose (Chapter 9). This relaxation story is called the Lotus Flower (Chapter 9). Take a deep breath in. Let out it. Let's begin...

Integrating Mindfulness Into Your Everyday Life

Science tells us that to experience the brain-changing benefits of mindfulness, we need to practice it ten minutes a day. It doesn't need to be a continuous ten minutes; it could be five minutes twice a day or even three minutes spread out throughout the day. But set aside the time, at the same time every day, if possible, to make it a habit. This habit will result in improved focus, connectedness with your child, reduced stress, and more resiliency. Think of this book as a toolbox full of tools you can use whenever you need them. To create a more mindful life, use the tools in this book often. Brain pathways are built by daily practice; if you don't use mindfulness, you will lose it.

Mindful breathing, movement, and awareness are some of the many activities covered in this book. These are important strategies that promote social and emotional learning that your child can practice every day. Following are some specific ways to establish these valuable habits.

Mindful Breathing

- **Make it a habit.** Encourage your child to engage in the breathing activities presented in Chapter 3 daily. Of all the activities in this book, breathing is especially important and a fundamental piece of mindfulness. Through breath, your child is able to take control of his nervous system. Breath work teaches children they can change how they feel with as little as ten deep breaths.
- **Do it anywhere!** Finding time to breathe doesn't mean you sit in a quiet place in a meditative position. While this may be ideal, it is not always practical. Encourage your child to practice breathing while riding in the car on the way to school, bicycle riding, or even walking to a friend's house. These random moments of mindful breathing will help to integrate it into your child's life.
- **Encourage kids to think of their breath in difficult times.** Your child can then utilize her breathing practice before a test at school, a speaking part in a play, or even before shooting a basket at a big game. Your child's breath is always with her and can be used whenever and wherever she needs it.

Mindful Awareness

- **Calm down.** If your child is needing to balance a high energy level, do Thunderstorm from Chapter 4 followed by Ambient Music (Chapter 4) and a breathing exercise. This will provide deep impact followed by a calming activity to level out energy levels.

- **Incorporate mindfulness into mealtimes by adding a mindful vegetable or mindful dessert exercise.** Have your child lead the mindful eating. It is difficult to eat an entire meal mindfully so just introduce it with a few bites or a dessert.
- **Before homework, practice a couple of the focus activities.** If your child is still rushing through homework or becoming frustrated with it, incorporate a few movement breaks coupled with listening activities. Remind him to be kind to himself by doing a few kindness activities as well. These activities will get his mind primed for learning.
- **Turn a mindless activity into a mindful one.** Most activities can contain a mindfulness component, but sometimes you need to be creative. Mornings are rushed for most families and there may not be as much time for mindfulness, so make it part of something your child is already doing. Have your child mindfully brush her teeth. This may require providing clues on the bathroom mirror, such as listen to the water, notice the taste, feel the toothbrush in your hands, smell and notice the color of the toothpaste. This activity will start your child's day with focus and mindfulness.

Kindness and Gratitude

- **Practice kindness and gratitude in a group.** Many of the activities in the kindness and gratitude section (Chapter 8) are meant to be completed as a family and some even outside the home setting. These activities invite your child to take action mindfully in the world. While some of these activities are harder to sequence into a daily practice, activities such as Volunteer Work, Pay It Forward, and Gratitude Walk, can be implemented weekly as a family. This practice expands kindness and gratitude, making them part of your family structure. Acts of kindness are meant to be shared with the world. Brainstorm ways to be kind as a family and reflect on why kindness is important. Nurturing mindfulness through positive social action results in emotional and cognitive growth in transformative ways.
- **Model kindness and gratitude.** Children learn by observing. Model the skills you want to instill in your children. The more they see you being kind and grateful, the more they will want to be kind and grateful. After all, kindness is contagious!

In closing, now that you have become familiar with the science, benefits, and activities to enhance mindfulness in your child's life, you can start to build a daily mindfulness practice for you and your child that you can take out into the world. Performing mindful acts off the mat builds our executive functioning skills, compassion, and self-esteem, which enables us to contribute to the world in a meaningful way. Go forth and be mindful!

Resources

Albers, S. (2009). *Eat, Drink, and Be Mindful: How to End Your Struggle with Mindless Eating and Start Savoring Food with Intention and Joy*. Oakland, CA: New Harbinger.

Black, D.S., Cole, S., Irwin, M.R., Breen, E., St. Cyr, N.M., Nazarian, N., & Lavretsky, H. (2013). "Yogic Meditation Reverses NF-ÐB and IRF-Related Transcriptome Dynamics in Leukocytes of Family Dementia Caregivers in a Randomized Controlled Trial." *Psychoneuroendocrinology*, 38(3), 348–355. http://doi.org/10.1016/j.psyneuen.2012.06.011.

Broad, W.J. (2012). *The Science of Yoga: The Risks and the Rewards*. New York, NY: Simon & Schuster, Inc.

Burke, C.A. (2009). "Mindfulness-Based Approaches with Children and Adolescents: A Preliminary Review of Current Research in an Emergent Field." *Journal of Child and Family Studies*, 19(2):133–144.

Cole, R. "Conditions for Calm." Retrieved from www.encognitive.com/files/Anatomy.pdf.

Cook, J. (2017). *Bubble Gum Brain*. Chattanooga, TN: National Center for Youth Issues.

Danzig, M.T. (2014). *Yoga for Busy Little Hands: Great for Kids with ADD, ADHD, Autism and in Classrooms*. Charleston, SC: Color Me Yoga Enterprises.

Davis, D., & Hayes, J. (2011). "What Are the Benefits of Mindfulness? A Practice Review of Psychotherapy-Related Research." *Psychotherapy, 48*(2), 198–208.

Davies, P., & Gavin, W.J. (2007). "Validating the Diagnosis of Sensory Processing Disorders Using EEG Technology." *American Journal of Occupational Therapy, 61*(2), 176–189.

Deak, J.A.M., & Ackerley, S. (2017). *Your Fantastic Elastic Brain: Stretch It, Shape It*. San Francisco, CA: Little Pickle Press.

Dennison, P.E. (1989). *Brain Gym: Teacher's Edition*. Edu-Kinesthetics, Inc.

Diamond, A., & Lee, K. (2011). "Interventions Shown to Aid Executive Function Development in Children 4 to 12 Years Old." *Science, 333*(6,045), 949–6,410.

Dweck, C.S., & Leggett, E.L. (1988). "A Social-Cognitive Approach to Motivation and Personality." *Psychological Review, 95*(2), 256–273.

Dweck, C.S., & Mueller, C.M. (1998). "Praise for Intelligence Can Undermine Children's Motivation and Performance." *Journal of Personality and Social Psychology* (75), 33–52.

Flynn, L. (2013). *Yoga for Children*. Avon, MA: Adams Media.

Gard, T., Taquet, M., Dixit, R., Hoelzel, B.K., Demontjoye, Y., Brach, N., & Lazar, S.W. (2014). "Fluid Intelligence and Brain Functional Organization in Aging Yoga and Meditation Practitioners." *Frontiers in Aging Neuroscience, 6*(76).

Goldberg, L. (2013). *Yoga Therapy for Children with Autism and Special Needs.* New York, NY: Norton & Company.

Gothe, N., Pontifex, M., Hillman, C., & McAuley, E. (2013). "Acute Effects of Yoga on Executive Function." *Journal of Physical Activity and Health, 10,* 488–495.

Hagen, I., & Nayar, U.S. (2014). "Yoga for Children and Young People's Mental Health and Well-Being: Research Review and Reflections on the Mental Health Potentials of Yoga." *Frontiers in Psychiatry, 5*(35).

Hannaford, C. (2013). *Smart Moves: Why Learning Is Not All in Your Head*. Salt Lake City, UT: Great River Books.

Hawn, G., Holden, W., & Bean, J. (2014). *10 Mindful Minutes*. Grand Haven, MI: Brilliance Audio.

Hirschi, G. (2016). *Mudras: Yoga in Your Hands*. Newburyport, MA: Weiser Books.

Innes, K.E., Selfe, T.K., Brown, C.J., Rose, K.M., & Thompson-Heisterman, A. (2012). "The Effects of Meditation on Perceived Stress and Related Indices of

Psychological Status and Sympathetic Activation in Persons with Alzheimer's Disease and Their Caregivers: A Pilot Study." *Evidence-Based Complementary and Alternative Medicine: eCAM*, 927509. http://doi.org/10.1155/2012/927509.

Jacobson, E. (1932). "Electrophysiology of Mental Activities." *American Journal of Psychology, 44*, 667–694.

Johnston, C.A., Tyler, C., Stansberry, S.A., Palcic, J.L., & Foreyt, J.P. (2009). "Gum Chewing Affects Academic Performance in Adolescents." ASN Scientific Sessions and Annual Meeting at Experimental Biology, New Orleans, LA, April 2009.

Kabat-Zinn, J. (1990). *Full Catastrophe Living: Using the Wisdom of Your Body and Mind to Face Stress, Pain, and Illness*. New York, NY: Delacourt.

Khalsa, S. (1999). *Fly Like a Butterfly: Yoga for Children*. Herndon, VA: Shining Circle.

Kranowitz, C. S. (2006). *The Out-of-Sync Child Has Fun: Activities for Kids with Sensory Integration Dysfunction*. New York, NY: Penguin Group.

Lavretsky, H., Siddarth, P., Nazarian, N., St. Cyr, N., Khalsa, D.S., Lin, J., & Irwin, M.R. (2013). "A Pilot Study of Yogic Meditation for Family Dementia Caregivers with Depressive Symptoms: Effects on Mental Health, Cognition, and Telomerase Activity." *International Journal of Geriatric Psychiatry, 28*(1), 57–65. http://doi.org/10.1002/gps.3790.

Mahar, M., Murphy S., Rowe D., et al. (2006). "Effects of a Classroom-Based Program on Physical Activity and On-Task Behavior." *Medicine and Science in Sports and Exercise, 38*(12), 2,086–2,094.

McCloud, C., & Messing, D. (2016). *Have You Filled a Bucket Today?: A Guide to Daily Happiness for Kids*. Brighton, MI: Bucket Fillosophy.

Mendelson, T., Greenberg, M.T., Dariotis, J.K., Feagans Gould, L., Rhoades, B.L., & Leaf, P.J. (2010). "Feasibility and Preliminary Outcomes of a School-Based Mindfulness Intervention for Urban Youth." *Journal of Abnormal Child Psychology, 38*, 985–994.

Napoli, M., Krech, P.R., & Holley, L.C. (2005). "Mindfulness Training for Elementary School Students." *Journal of Applied School Psychology, 21*(1).

Newberg, A., Wintering, N., Khalsa, D.S., Roggenkamp, H., & Waldman, M. (2010). "Meditation Effects on Cognitive Function and Cerebral Blood Flow in Subjects with Memory Loss: A Preliminary Study." *Journal of Alzheimer's Disease, 20*, 517–526.

Rey, H.A., & Krasinski, J. (2016). *Curious George*. Boston, MA: Houghton Mifflin Harcourt.

Rosenblatt, L.E., Gorantla, S., Torres, J.A., Yarmush, R.S., Rao, S., Park, E.R., & Levine, J.B. (2011). "Relaxation Response–Based Yoga Improves Functioning in Young Children with Autism: A Pilot Study." *The Journal of Alternative and Complementary Medicine, 17*(11), 1,029–1,035.

Saltzman, A. (2014). *A Still Quiet Place: A Mindfulness Program for Teaching Children and Adolescents to Ease Stress and Difficult Emotions*. Oakland, CA: New Harbinger.

Sarris, J., Kean, J., Schweitzer, I., & Lake, J. (2011). "Complementary Medicines (Herbal and Nutritional Products) in the Treatment of Attention Deficit Hyperactivity Disorder (ADHD): A Systematic Review of the Evidence." *Complementary Therapies in Medicine, 19*(4), 216–227.

Sears, W. (2009). *The NDD Book: How Nutrition Deficit Disorder Affects Your Child's Learning, Behavior, and Health, and What You Can Do about It—Without Drugs*. New York, NY: Little, Brown.

Singleton, O., Hölzel, B.K., Vangel, M., Brach, N., Carmody, J., & Lazar, S.W. (2014). "Change in Brainstem Gray Matter Concentration Following a Mindfulness-Based Intervention Is Correlated with Improvement in Psychological Well-Being." *Frontiers in Human Neuroscience*, www.frontiersin.org/articles/10.3389/fnhum.2014.00033/full.

The Hawn Foundation (2011). *The MindUP Curriculum: Brain-Focused Strategies for Learning—and Living. Grades Pre-K–2*. New York, NY: Scholastic Teaching Resources.

Yolen, J., & Teague, M. (2006). *How Do Dinosaurs Eat Their Food?* New York, NY: HarperCollins Publishers.

Index

I

K

L

M

N

O

T

V

W

Y

Z